LITERATURE
A CRASH
COURSE

LITERATURE
A CRASH
COURSE
CORY BELL

WATSON-GUPTILL
PUBLICATIONS
New York

Library of Congress Catalog Card Number: 98-89370

ISBN 0-8230-0980-7

This book was conceived, designed, and produced by
THE IVY PRESS LIMITED
2/3 St Andrews Place
Lewes, East Sussex. BN7 1UP

Art Director: PETER BRIDGEWATER
Editorial Director: SOPHIE COLLINS
Designer: JANE LANAWAY
Managing Editor: ANNE TOWNLEY
Page layout: CHRIS LANAWAY
Picture research: VANESSA FLETCHER
Illustrations: ALAN and GILL BRIDGEWATER

Reproduction and printing in Hong Kong by
Hong Kong Graphic & Printing Ltd.

1 2 3 4 5 / 03 02 01 00 99

Contents

Introduction

Classic but still controversial: England's greatest epic poet, John Milton (see p. 32).

(see p. 32)

Timeline

More of a contextual chronology than a timeline, because authors and movements are constantly overlapping. A selected list of major events happening at the time the authors were living, to illuminate the world they inhabited: Racine wrote *Phèdre* just as the dodo was becoming extinct; and *Madame Bovary* appeared the year after Pasteur discovered germs.

LITERATURE is simply the list of books that people think will always be rewarding to the imagination. No two people agree where this list starts and stops, since everyone's reading experience is different. What complicates matters is that the list making is principally done by other writers. And writers, of course, lean on other writers— look up to them, steal from them, or try to pigeonhole them. They call the results a "literary tradition."

The pleasures of the imagination: a reader of Rousseau, as painted by Wright of Derby.

THE PLOT THICKENS

What's happening between some well-known covers; what's happening somewhere else in the literary world; what literary lingo means. This survey of literature is intentionally **lateral:** *broad, that is, rather than deep. Result is, you may encounter just about anything within these inserts!*

That's why Edmund Spenser's enormous Elizabethan poem, The Faerie Queene, *is "literature," while the novels of Jeffrey Archer aren't—not yet, anyway. Archer's readers must outnumber Spenser's by a million to one these days; but Spenser's melodious allegories were to influence Shakespeare and Milton, while Archer's easy-write, easy-read manner has so far won very little respect from fellow scribblers.*

We are all entitled to disagree with the consensus of writers as to what constitutes literature— disagreeing is a vital way of working out our own values. There isn't any true consensus anyway: for instance, Tolstoy—generally reckoned one of the pinnacles of the scribbling profession—thought that Shakespeare—generally reckoned another—was completely worthless. I certainly don't find every writer

Superscribbler Leo Tolstoy (1828–1910), a one-man literary industry (see p. 62).

Gorky reads to Stalin. Writing's connections with political power form a leading theme in literary history.

mentioned in this Crash Course equally attractive, as you'll see; but I think it's interesting, as a matter of curiosity, to explore the shape of this thing they call "the tradition" or "the canon."

What we have here, in effect, are some of the main features of the literary map as it appears to writers of English at the end of the 20th century. (That, of course, includes a vast amount that has been translated from other languages.) To emphasize, we're talking about imaginative writing—the kind that lets your mind float free on another plane from here and now; that lets you rethink how things are and might be. Stories and

MEMO

Literature is bound together by recommendations. These are the author's personal ones. They may lead you to great new discoveries—or you might fundamentally disagree.

poems and, to a lesser extent, the criticism that revolves around them, rather than information and instructions. That's why the Bible doesn't appear, for all its majestic "literary" qualities: before and beyond those, it's a book of instructions on how to live.

Also, we're talking principally about imaginative reading. Writing designed for public performance appears here only if it still looks good when you read it in private; if you really want the stage, not the page, turn to the Crash Course on theater.

The great and the good of modern literature: Virginia Woolf and James Joyce (below).

CORY BELL

How this course works

Each double-page spread is devoted to an author, a literary movement, or a group of works with something in common, and the story proceeds more or less chronologically. On each spread there are some regular features. It won't take you long to figure them out, but check the boxes on pages 8–11 for more information.

800 B.C. The Greeks adopt the Phoenician consonantal alphabet. With an additional five vowels, the full alphabet emerges.

776 B.C. The first recorded Olympic games; they will continue intermittently for 1,000 years and then lapse until 1896.

588 B.C. The Cloaca Maxima, the great sewer of Rome, is constructed. It will be open to the air until Augustus encloses it in 33 B.C.

800~400 B.C.

It's All Greek
Homer and the Tragedians

The gods descending on humanity: the Homeric theme on a Greek vase.

This idea called literature gets going around the 8th century B.C., in Greece, when two long-verse stories about long-dead ancestors are set down in writing. Sword-wielding tribes the world over once listened to "epics" like these. But pen-wielding, when it occurred in the ancient world, was largely the preserve of priests—with their do's, don'ts and this-is-how-it-is's. As a result, stories are fused with instructions and doctrines in the Bible and in the great Indian poems, the Mahabharata *and* Ramayana. *But what's crucial about their Greek equivalents, the* Iliad *and* Odyssey, *is that the writer leaves the imagination free. You can believe it on whatever level you like: it's simply "literature."*

Gilgamesh rendered in Assyrian sculpture, c. 725 B.C.—shortly before his legend faded from memory.

Homer—whether a blind bard from the island of Kos (the traditional version), a brand name for a bunch of traditions (the "analytic" revision) or a master transformer of traditional material (the *revised* revision)—sets the terms for literature because he knows all the tricks. Like any storyteller's, his job is to spin it out but stop them yawning: delay the fall of Troy while Achilles sulks in his tent; send Odysseus home to Ithaca across the length of the known world; cast out the long hexameter lines in massive, extended "Homeric metaphors." But keep it vivid, keep it varied: flesh out every action and actor; alternate lofty and intimate, savage and sweet. "Literary effects" are chiefly effects defined by Homer: over the last four centuries, ancient and modern critics have agreed that first equals best.

MEMO

The most exciting English versions of Homer (the world's most translated poet) are by George Chapman (1616) and Christopher Logue, who adapted the *Iliad*—check out his *War Music* (1981).

538 B.C. Public libraries are in use in Athens. Aristotle is credited with establishing the earliest large Greek library in the 4th century B.C.

500 B.C. The Hindu medical work, the *Sushruta Samhita*, describes plastic surgery techniques used in the repair and creation of noses.

400 B.C. London is founded on the banks of the Thames River, when the Celtic King Belin builds a mud wall around a few dozen huts.

Call that nostalgic? Well, nostalgia's built in: Homer's nostalgic for a distant past when men were heroes and gods walked and talked with them. Hesiod, maybe a century later, mourns the Age of Gold and curses the present Age of Iron. Poets in his wake try to get the ear of those gods or to reason with them. Like the Book of Job in the Bible, the Athenian tragedies explore the wounds of human experience—if the gods are good, why do we get this trash?—and heal them with great poetry (the process Aristotle called "catharsis"). *ÆSCHYLUS* (525–456 B.C.), in his trilogy the *Oresteia*, followed by

THE PLOT THICKENS

Literature is largely a bunch of Greek terms. Not only "poetry," "prose," and "tragedy" but also "comedy"—see rude, satirizing **Aristophanes** *(c. 448–380 B.C.); "odes"—see* **Pindar** *(c. 522–443 B.C.), who turned them out for Olympic victors; and "lyrics"—see the beautiful short poems of* **Sappho of Lesbos** *(6th century B.C.)—who lent her name to other things besides.*

Floodlit

The earliest known epic is *Gilgamesh*, recorded in Sumeria from the second millennium B.C. The majestic, fatalistic story of the eponymous hero includes an account of the biblical Flood. A version written on clay tablets was discovered in the 19th century on the site of Nineveh in Iraq.

SOPHOCLES (496–406 B.C.), handing Oedipus his complex, and *EURIPIDES* (480–406 B.C.), who moves from the passions of *Medea* (431 B.C.) to the *Bacchae*'s meditations on ecstasy and violence (406 B.C.), all use available means—a clutch of "protagonists" set against a chorus of women, in a single continuous action—for the deepest imaginative effect.

The traditional image of Homer (blind bard), singing by the gates of Athens, as imagined by an 18th-century French painter. Little is known about him for certain but the myth survives.

| 221 B.C. In Alexandria, Eristratus names the heart valves, figures out how blood flows, and describes the convolutions of the brain. | 63 B.C. Marcus Tullius Tiro of Rome invents a system of Latin shorthand that will be used for over a thousand years. | c. 5 B.C. Heron, the prolific Alexandrian inventor, designs temple doors that open automatically. | | A.D. 1 The world population is about 250 million. |

250 B.C.~A.D. 150

The Augustan and the Disgusting
Writers of the Roman Empire

Æneas arrives at the court of Queen Dido.

*"Roman literature is Greek literature written in Latin,"
wrote the historian Heinrich von Treitschke—and he
had a point. The Romans imitated their cultural
forebears fawningly. PLAUTUS (c. 254–184 B.C.) and
TERENCE (c. 190–159 B.C.) took on comedy; SENECA
(4 B.C.–A.D. 65) tragedy, while VIRGIL (70–19 B.C.)
modeled himself on the pastoral poems of the Greek
Theocritus in his* Eclogues, *before setting out to be
Roma's Homer. His poem lifts the Trojan prince Æneas out of the* Iliad
*and lands him—via a dalliance with Queen Dido of Carthage—in Italy,
where his descendants would found Rome, and eventually, under the
Emperor Augustus (Virgil's patron), achieve cosmic supremacy. Though
the Æneid was Western Europe's favorite epic until the 18th century (the
Church loved Virgil, thinking his* Fourth Eclogue *prophesied Christ), its
heavy, unctuous grandeur tends to weary modern readers.*

Virgil is more likable when he evokes
Italian country life in the *Georgics*,
which is almost a verse manual: how to
keep bees, prune vines, and so on. More
amiable yet is
Virgil's friend
HORACE (65–8 B.C.),
writing his four
books of *Odes* in a
country villa
donated by his
patron Mæcenas,
perfecting the tone
we now call
"civilized"—fond

MEMO

Try Peter Whigham's
dazzling translations of
Catullus; or the
companionable, droll
tale spinning of *The
Golden Ass* by Apuleius
(A.D. 125–after 170), as
rendered by Robert
Graves.

Follically challenged
Horace and ivy-browed
Virgil hear out fellow poet

Varius, chez Mæcenas. A
handy wax tablet contains
the poetic composition.

A.D. 100 The composition of the *Kama Sutra*, a Hindu treatise written in Sanskrit on the art of love, is begun in India.

A.D. 105 A Chinese court official, Ts'ai Lun, succeeds in making paper from vegetable fibers. The secret method of paper making will be kept for 500 years.

THE PLOT THICKENS

Classical critics defined the different meters for verse, splitting lines down into types of "feet," such as "iambs" (light syllable then heavy syllable) and "trochees" (vice versa). These terms have been adopted in English, but for rhythms of stress which classical verse didn't have. For the English, "Watch my in-laws abseil in through windows!" is a line of five trochees (stress-unstress); for the Greeks, who reckoned by vowel-length ("quantity"), it would instead be five iambs (short-long)—or an "iambic pentameter."

The Art of Love: a Pompeian muralist gives a hot rendition of Ovid's theme. He was widely read in his day, but later reviled by the Christian Church.

Oh, Cynthia!
Sextus Propertius (c. 50–c. 16 B.C.), Ovid's mentor, is the most demanding and the most emotionally sophisticated of Roman poets; his odes to "Cynthia" became a particular favorite with 20th-century poets such as Ezra Pound.

of his pleasures but self-controlled, worldly wise but self-deprecating. Both of these "Augustan" poets are ultra-scrupulous literary craftsmen, setting a model of sonorous elegance in verse. They're closely followed by *OVID* (43 B.C.–A.D. 18), the man-about-Rome, wit, and philanderer of *Amores* and *The Art of Love*, the picturesque legend weaver of the *Metamorphoses*, who unaccountably fell foul of Augustus and ended his days in exile by the Black Sea.

The *exciting* end, however, of Roman writing is when the clever and tender shades into the vicious and gross, for which see *CATULLUS* (c. 84–c. 54 B.C.). He was earlier than these Augustans, and, in his love poems to "Lesbia" or his filthy invective, much more emotionally meaty. "Satire" was in fact the Romans' chief contribution to the jargon of literature: Horace wrote satires and, after him, *MARTIAL* (A.D. 40–104), in his epigrams, and *JUVENAL* (A.D. 60–136) made a fine art of foul-tongued rudeness. The same sensibility comes through in the most extraordinary remnant of Roman fiction— the fragments called the *Satyricon*, by Nero's courtier *PETRONIUS* (d. A.D. 65). Mixing prose and verse, grotesquerie, sophistication, and realism, loads of sex, and loads of food, it belongs to a culture of exuberant, free-form literary experiment.

770 The Japanese produce the first mass publication, a block-printed Buddhist prayer.

1000 The coast of Nova Scotia is discovered by the Norse explorer Leif Ericson. His exploits will be celebrated in the 13th-century Icelandic Sagas.

1086 The *Domesday Book*, an inventory and assessment of landed property in England, is compiled at the order of William I.

1120 An Arab traveler visiting southern Russia notes how a man "binds to his feet the thigh-bones of oxen," an early example of skates.

600~1300
The Bitter North
From Beowulf to the Nibelungenlied

After a hard day's arson, pillage, and looting, the Germanic tribes who trashed the Roman Empire liked to gather in the evening to quaff and hear verse. Old English poetry is a prime example. Similar to a country & western bar, this was a case of guys getting gloomy together, sobbing into their mead at the miseries of life, and the mysterious ways of wyrd, fate. Hwæt! the poet strikes up, setting into an insistent, alliterative rhythm—listen, here's the plaint of the exiled, icicled Seafarer, rowing his way across the North Sea; here's The Ruin, crumbling walls of some Roman city, "work of giants," don't make 'em like that anymore.

The 9th-century manuscript of *Beowulf*.

THE PLOT THICKENS

Ireland—the center of learning in Dark Age Europe—produced its nearest approach to an epic in the Tain Bó Cuailgne (recorded 12th century), introducing figures like Cuchulain, Conchobar, Deirdre, and Medb. Welsh verse of perhaps the sixth century comes from the semilegendary Taliesin and Aneirin. The manuscript Book of Aneirin contains an elegy for the Welsh chieftains who were killed by the Saxons at Cattraeth, and features the earliest mention of King Arthur.

Here, above all, are the grim and stirring deeds of Beowulf, the Danish hero, grappling with the monster Grendel at the bottom of a bog and then—even worse—having to confront Grendel's mother. Like country & western, again, there's an undertow of down-in-the-mouth dirty humor, as in the riddles: "It hangs stiff and hard, under a man's clothes, waiting to fit a familiar hole …" (A key, stupid.)

Maybe, though, this mead-hall jukebox impression misleads. Some of what survives must have been written by sophisticated literati, lending their compositions a nostalgic clangorous edge as a kind of verbal half-timbering.

1226 Francis of Assissi sees a vision of an angel just before he dies.

1290 Spectacles are invented; Italian artist Tommaso da Modena will depict an elderly churchman wearing them in a fresco at Treviso in 1352.

Notably, the *Dream of the Rood* (i.e., the cross) uses the verse format for an extraordinary mystical vision, voiced by the instrument of crucifixion. In fact the Anglo-Saxons, like the Romans before them, were highly concerned with being civilized—as is clear from the prefaces Alfred gave to his translations from Latin authors (in the 890s). Alfred, the first real English king, is also the first real English prose writer.

The literary epicenter of Dark Age Europe, however, is way offshore—in Iceland. Among the glaciers, geysers, and lava, Viking scribes of the 10th century commit to parchment the folk memories of ancient Teutonic myth in the poems of the *Edda*; slightly later, an extraordinarily tough, realistic prose tradition develops in the *Sagas* (i.e., "stories"). Factual material is woven into tight and gripping action narrative, notably in the writing of *Snorri* STURLUSON

Cædmon the monk

The oldest Old English poet to bear a name is Cædmon, who composed a "Hymn of Creation" in the 670s in Northumbria. The story goes that he was an uneducated herdsman tending his flock when he received the gift of music in a vision, and later produced several long poems based on the scriptures.

Caedmon is divinely inspired to write his songs and verse.

Forging the sword for Nordic hero Siegfried: 12th-century Norwegian woodcarving.

(1178–1241) and in the novel-length *Njal's Saga*. A similarly dry, laconic, "life's like that" edge colors another adaptation of Teutonic legend, the protracted, fierce-battles-and-fair-maidens of the *Nibelungenlied*, composed in Germany c.1300 (later immortalized in Wagner's music dramas *Der Ring des Nibelungen*).

Gnomic garden

Penning Old English poetry's peanuts. Think of three words, threaded by sound: build your line around them ... with a break in its breadth. Rhyme is redundant, reason is rambling. Frost sceal freosan, fyr wudu meltan ('frost shall freeze, fire melt wood': a "gnomic verse," gnawing on gnarled clichés).

850 Coffee is discovered (supposedly) by Kaldi, an Abyssinian goatherd. It will be introduced into Europe in the mid 17th century.

1096-99 The first Crusade; the Crusaders will take Jerusalem in 1099.

1145 A bridge is built across the Danube at Stratisbon.

200~1400

Asian Exports
The Great Storytellers

Scribblers, before modern times, weren't over-concerned with inventing original stories. Like jewelers, they were expected to cut, polish, and set materials brought in from somewhere else. That somewhere else, for European writers, was very frequently Asia—above all the great story factory of India. Shakespeare, Chaucer, and Dante all draw on narrative ideas that can be ultimately traced back, through complex transmissions, to the oral art of Indian village-square entertainers—much of it recorded in the great 2d-century collection called the Panchatantra. *The most familiar Western image of this Asian art is Scheherezade, spinning her yarns to keep the ax from her neck for the* 1001

Bookishness, Persian-style: a 16th-century *madrasa*, as seen in one of Iran's great illuminated manuscripts.

Arabian Nights. *But Sinbad, Aladdin, Ali Baba, and the rest probably started in the subcontinent, or possibly Iran, rather than Haroun ar-Rashid's Baghdad. The collection gradually traveled west, translation by translation, finally hitting Europe in the 18th century.*

Anyway, literary Arabs feel about the Western reputation of the *Arabian Nights* the way Westerners might feel if Arabs took Walt Disney for the West's highest cultural achiever. (Perhaps he is?) Classic literature, for them, is the grand, rolling phrases and manly passions of the pre-Islamic odes collected as the *Mu'allakat* (a style overshadowed by the supreme grandeur of the Qur'an), and the poems of *MUTANABBI* (915-65). For modern Westerners, the difficulty with this poetry is its unfamiliar sense of form and pace. Like the slow, sweet, sensuousness of the Indian *Gita Govinda*, it can seem just one damn

1202 Leonardo Fibonacci's (c. 1170–1245) *Liber Abbaci* is a mathematical treatise introducing the Hindu-Arabic system of numerals using ten symbols.

1270 17-year-old Marco Polo begins his embassy from the Pope to Kublai, Grand Khan of Tartary. He will not return to Venice until 1295.

c.1332 The first outbreak of the Black Death (bubonic plague) in India. By 1351, it will have claimed 75 million lives worldwide.

beauty after another, on and on and on. Seeking the building-and-developing format of the Western classics, Edward Fitzgerald translated Omar Khayyam's *Rubaiyat* (or "Quatrains") as a structured sequence, something Omar never intended back in the Nishapur of A.D. 1200. Nonetheless, the personality of the Persian astronomer shines through: wine loving, fate fearing, shoulder shrugging about religion, he is the most quotable and most cynical of companions. More lyrical, more mystical, the *Divan* of the later HAFIZ (1320–91) is more highly regarded by Iranian tradition: a collection of short *ghazals* or *ghasels*, about love, flowers, wine, and nightingales.

THE PLOT THICKENS

The masterpiece of Iranian poetry is the epic Shahnama of Firdousi: 35 years in the writing (976–1011), five times as long as the Iliad, and telling of Iran's great emperors. It is best known in the West for the tragic combat of Rustam with his son Sohrab (as adapted by Matthew Arnold).

Quite another sense of structure comes through in reading the lyric poetry of East Asia. Spareness, brevity, breathiness: think of the way the brush hits the scroll for a few dazzling strokes in Chinese painting, leaving the whole sheet charged with imaginative mystery. The poems of *Wang Wei* (699–759) and *Li Po* (701–762) are like that—a bare handful of images thrust forward, leaving a scent of refined but impassioned nostalgia in the air.

The Japanese—masters of bonsai gardening—pare down this Chinese art to produce the minimal, seventeen-syllable poem, the *haiku*. This refined sensibility is also cultivated in *The Pillow Book of Sei Shonagon* and the extraordinary *Tale of Genji* (see also p. 36). This wealth of material would only reach Europe in the 20th century, in translations such as Arthur Waley's.

Snow on the willow-boughs, confidences in the courtyard: the world of the *Tale of Genji*, as seen by a 17th-century illustrator.

1000 Ethelred II decrees that any merchants who want to trade in London have to pay a tax in peppercorns.

1295 Marco Polo brings spices, Asian recipes, and— the story goes—pasta back to Italy; the latter will become a staple of the Italian diet.

c.1295 The Harrowing of Hell, one of the earliest known English miracle plays, is performed.

1000~1450

The Ladies and the Gents
The Rise of Courtly Love

Battlefield clashes in *The Song of Roland*.

Forget the hippies: "Make love not war" was a concept of the 12th century. Prior to then, Europe had been in a prolonged bad mood. Men went around pursuing each other in dastardly fashion with jagged shards of metal, and their poems reflected this—stuff like the 11th-century French epic The Song of Roland, *the Spanish poem of the* Cid, *and the English fragment called* The Battle of Maldon *(c.1000). These chansons de gestes ("songs of deeds")—particularly* Roland—*can be finely controlled, terse, driving narratives; but life in them consists chiefly of battlefield boasts, buddy bonding, and sword blades clashing.*

Then: step forward *Chrétien DE TROYES,* c. 1170, with his rhyming verse romances. And the battlefield yields ground to the love-bower, men's allegiances shift from brave commanders to fair damsels. Fantasy, charm, and wit are the

Lancelot rides out with Guinevere: 14th-century French illumination.

order of the day: Chrétien was writing for a new, mixed-sex court audience, with tastes sophisticated by the Eastern encounters of the Crusades. A culture of *courtoisie,* defined by the adoration of ladies, is effectively his creation; it would be epitomized by the long, allegorical *Roman de la Rose,* started by *Guillaume DE LORRIS* (c.1230) and finished by *Jean MEUNG* (c.1275). But the stuff of CdT's romances is what his near-contemporary Jean Bodel would call "the Matter of Britain"—that is, the sprawl of tall and tangled tales associated with King Arthur.

Arthur wanders off the pages of some very unsound history books into verse about 1150, in the hands of the Jerseyman Wace.

1305 In Padua, Giotto paints frescoes depicting the Last Judgment and the lives of Christ and the Virgin Mary in Santa Maria dell'Arena.

1313 Bernard Schwarz, a German grayfriar, invents gunpowder.

1317 Salic Law, excluding women from succession to the throne, is adopted in France.

The Green Knight presents his head, removed at his own request by Sir Gawain, to King Arthur.

The "Matter" doesn't by any means end there: *Sir Gawain and the Green Knight*, written in alliterative verse by Anon. in northwestern England c.1375, stands, alongside Chaucer, as the richest long poem in English before *Paradise Lost*.

It shifts from the uncanny (Green Knight, severed head in hand, riding before King Arthur and his Round Table) to the picturesque (evoking the since-vanished forests of Britain), the amatory (as Gawain tries to resist his seductive hostess), and, finally, to the wryly humane, as Gawain sneaks a kiss and half loses his honor.

Coitus reservatus

"Courtoisie" was devoted to ladies' "honor"; thus in the poem, Parzival shares a bed with a naked maiden without touching her. In actual practice, this meant that suitors were committed to lovemaking without ejaculation.

Wace spurs the Englishman Layamon soon after to compose the interminable alliterative epic *Brut*, which surely must be one of the nadirs of English poetry (we at *Crash Course* have had to study the damn thing). But it's the storylines in the "Matter of Britain" springing from deep in Welsh mythology (such as the 13th-century *Mabinogion*) that inspire the most challenging romances, from writers over in Germany: Gottfried of Strassburg's *Tristan* (c.1210) and Wolfram von Eschenbach's complex and spiritual *Parzival* (1200–12), concerning the Grail legend.

THE PLOT THICKENS

The grand summation of the whole Arthurian caboodle, everything from Merlin and Uther Pendragon to Sir Bedivere and Avalon done in ringing high-toned prose, is **Thomas Malory's** Morte d'Arthur—*written right at the end of the Middle Ages (c.1450–70), one of the first books Caxton printed with the technology that would revolutionize book production and massively expand book consumption.*

1250 An early encyclopedia, called *Speculum naturale, historiale, doctrinale,* is written by Vincent of Beauvais.

1266 England's bakers are told to mark their bread with trademarks so that if a faulty loaf turns up, they'll know whom to blame.

1275 An account of human dissection is published by William of Saliceto. The practice is discouraged by the Church.

1250~1320

Mount Dante
Approaching the Divine

If literature could be shown as a world map, Dante's Divine Comedy would have to be Mount Everest, for several reasons. First, on any test of quality, Dante ALIGHIERI (1265–1321) is one of the world's supreme versifiers—moving from magnificence to intimacy, from vivid visions to caustic epigrams with total command, able to make the simplest image bear the most complex weight. Secondly, he is one of the most ambitious, designing a poetic structure that would incorporate the complete intellectual, moral, and emotional experience of the world he knew.

Dante, as depicted in a 15th-century panel. His supremacy in Italian writing has always been recognized.

Thirdly, to writers looking back in time, this design would make the Divine Comedy *(c. 1307–21) seem the peak nearest to heaven—the most cohesive religious vision to be found outside Scripture.*

For the love of Beatrice

As well as in the *Divine Comedy*, Dante tells the story of his passion for Beatrice in the prose-and-verse, fact-and-vision structure of *La Vita Nuova* (1290–94).

Now, any fool can quote you the opening lines. *Nel mezzo del cammin di nostra vita …* In the middle of the path of our life [i.e., age 35], I found myself within a dark wood: Dante relates how, suffering from a midlife crisis, he dreams he meets Virgil—top poet, for Dante's times—who leads him off on a journey down through the *Inferno*. And many a fool can quote you Paolo and Francesca, the damned illicit lovers he meets whirling around the abyss in *Canto 5*—brought there by reading too much romantic literature.

1285 Smog becomes a problem in London as citizens burn soft coal to provide heat.

1310 The first brandy is distilled by French medical professor Arnaldus de Villa Nova.

1320 Pietro Cavallini paints frescoes for the Church of Santa Maria Donnaregina.

It's a bit classier to cite the Wood of Suicides in *Canto 11*, and really quite impressive to report back from *Canto 33*, where Count Ugolino and the Archbishop of Pisa are stuck forever up to their throats in ice, gnawing at each other's heads. (Political adversaries of Dante's; filling Hell gives you a great opportunity for settling scores, and Dante sure grabs it.) But how many get past the next canto—the bottom of the pit, where Judas writhes headfirst in Satan's mouth, to start the upward and outward climb through *Purgatorio*? Do yourself a favor, and struggle up to the top of that hill, where D. reencounters his lost love, Beatrice, who will lead him up through the heavenly spheres of *Paradiso* to the astonishing vision of the divine that culminates the hundred cantos.

A conversation with Justinian; in the *Divine Comedy, Canto 6,* *Paradiso.* Illustration from the Biblioteca Marciana, Venice.

> ### THE PLOT THICKENS
>
> *The nearest English equivalent to the Divine Comedy is Piers Plowman by* **William Langland**—*another visionary critique of the world, as seen by a cantankerous, individualistic member of England's Awkward Squad, but not that hot a poet. The nearest in terms of approach to Dante's quality and vision is the short poem Pearl, by the same Anon. who gave you Sir Gawain (see p. 21).*

On the other hand, there really is no world map of literature, and there are other, equally attractive ways of approaching heaven besides Dante's. In Konya in Turkey, 40 years before Dante loses sight of Beatrice, the Persian Sufi teacher *Jalaluddin RUMI* (1207–73) is pining for another lost love—the mysterious young man he calls Shams-i-Tabriz. He pours his spiritualized passion into the dazzling, exultant, psychologically piercing *Divan* (i.e., collection of odes), and summarizes his often strikingly modern insights in the *Mathnawi*—massive, multinarrated and meandering (Western ideas of structure definitely aren't at home here).

1201 The St. Gotthard Pass is opened in the Swiss Alps, linking the cantons of Uri and Ticino.

1247 The city of Buda is founded to replace the city of Pest that the Vandals had destroyed six years previously.

1309 Construction of the Doge's Palace in Venice begins. It won't be completed until 1483.

1366 In Europe, the main meal of the day is eaten at 9 o'clock in the morning.

1200~1450

Lutes and Lowlife
Petrarch, Boccaccio, and Chaucer

Lust looks like love when set in 14 lines
And has since Petrarch coined this type of verse.
Laura was the lady on whom he had designs.
He met her in Provence, where troubadours rehearse
The forms of stanza, based on patterned rhymes,
In which the poets of Europe would immerse
Themselves, as rhymeless ancient verse declines—
These troubs peak around 1200. Petrarch's terse
And shapely sonnet—octave, then sestina
(I.e. this here) comes later: it's no sweat
For eyeties like himself, exiled in Avignon.
For Anglos such as Shakespeare rhyme comes meaner.
They do three quatrains, then two lines rimed in set,
Unless like me they're smart. (Just having you on.)

François Villon
Thief, cutthroat, drunkard, pimp, and scrounger: great poet. He wanders in and out of jail through the 1450s, disappearing after a pardon from the gallows. He leaves *Le Grand Testament*, unmatched for gross ribaldry and humane pathos by anything between Catullus and Donne.

Villon, the notorious Sorbonne student.

W ell, PETRARCH (1304–74) is somewhat better than that. But he's got a lot to answer for: not only the sonnet but also, through his "humanist" studies, the poshing up of literature through classical allusion that would flavor European verse for five centuries. His friend BOCCACCIO (1313–75) helped these studies, but is better known for the first great piece of Italian prose, the *Decameron*. In the "ten days" of the title a gathering of Florentines, fleeing a plague in the city, tell each other a hundred lively, raunchy tales

Geoff directing the pilgrims down the highway to Canterbury. Illustration from the Ellesmere manuscript of his famously entertaining poem.

1400 The Hospital of St. Mary of Bethlehem (or Bedlam) becomes England's first hospital for the mentally ill. Bedlam will come to mean "a confused uproar."

1401 *De haeretico comburendo*—English statute authorizing the burning of witches. The last execution of witches among English-speaking people will occur in 1722.

A manuscript illustration to Boccaccio captures the workaday, matter-of-fact feel of his fiction, supposedly related by Florentines in exile.

reader-friendly masterpiece *Troilus and Criseyde* (late 1380s). But *The Canterbury Tales* (1387–1400), tripping along for the most part in light, persuasive couplets, extends on Boccaccio's range of tone.

Mixing high tales and low, depending on the teller, it makes each contribution act as part of a repartee between the Canterbury-bound pilgrims, thus creating a cohesive image of society from top to bottom—the model on which other English cultural figureheads like Shakespeare and Dickens would be elevated to "national" significance.

> **Troubadours**
>
> Troubadouring (or *Minnesang*, in Germany) was largely a lifestyle for 12th-century aristos on the loose. They went from court to court, pleading their passions for some lady of the house as piercingly as possible. A *jongleur* accompanist might twang the lute. Wackiness was part of the act: the Provençal Peire Vidal dressed as a wolf, and had hounds set on him, to prove his love for a lady named Louve (she-wolf).

about a world of princesses, monks, merchants, and servant girls—all ruled by sex and greed, all due for a comeuppance.

Hey, what a great literary device! An exceptionally well-read English government clerk picks up on it, adapts it, and creates the biggest, liveliest, and funniest poem in his language. *Geoffrey* CHAUCER (c.1343–1400) had already demonstrated his unique tone of tender empathy and wry, comic skepticism in the

In French poetry, meanwhile, top and bottom keep well apart. In the upper ranks: *Charles* of ORLEANS (1394–1465), penning sad *ballades* from an English jail after Agincourt, and *Christine* DE PISAN (1365–c.1430), protofeminist. Down in the dumps: *François* VILLON (1431–63?), the most searingly personal voice of his age; see box. (Unless, for total contrast, you go to the fresh-eyed love-and-nature lyrics of the 14th-century Welsh Dafydd ap Gwilym.)

1518 The conquistadores in Central America see prostitutes chewing gum, or chicle, the thick milky liquid from the sapodilla tree.

1519-22 First circumnavigation of the globe.

1535 The Galapagos (tortoise) Islands are discovered by the Spanish; a haven for buccaneers and whalers, they will be annexed by Ecuador in 1832.

1500~1615

Noble Poesy, Vulgar Prose
Renaissance Epics

As the hand-copied manuscript peters into obsolescence, and Gutenberg turns literature into mass industry, the Scottish poet William DUNBAR (1456–1513) is re-enlivening Chaucer's mix of high allegory and low scurrility, adding a grim sharpness of diction all his own. He heads a gang of fellow "Scottish Chaucerians," notably Robert Henryson. But Dunbar, dying at Flodden, stands at the turn of an age.

The court rhymesters of Europe, during the Renaissance, were offering up ever more extravagantly grandiose verbiage to reflect glory on their sumptuous patrons. *Lodovico ARIOSTO* (1474–1535), for example, going bananas for the Este Dukes of Ferrara in his picturesque variation on the tale of Roland, *Orlando Furioso* (1532). Or *Luis DE CAMOËNS* (1524–80), in Lisbon, dressing up in epic form the exploits of the Portuguese (who, it's true, had plenty to celebrate, having opened up the seas from India to Brazil) in *The Lusiads* (1572). Or *Edmund SPENSER* (1552–99), embroidering the ornate allegories of *The Faerie Queene* (1589) in praise of Queen Elizabeth.

Nymphs and shepherds

Pastoral—the "let's be shepherds" genre, derived from the Greek Theocritus via Virgil's *Eclogues*—was big in the 16th century; for an example that turns *considerably* weird ("let's now be women"), try Philip Sidney's *Arcadia* (1580s). Sidney is also famed as the lyric poet of the sonnet sequence *Astrophel and Stella*.

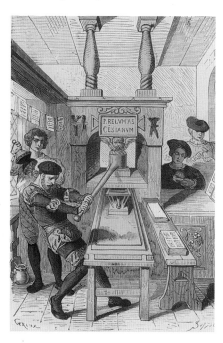

The hard grind of mass-produced literature. A 16th-century printing press in Paris.

1565 Konrad von Gesner (1516–65), Swiss physician and naturalist, refers to "a writing instrument consisting of a piece of lead in a wooden casing"—the humble pencil.

1575 The potato is cultivated in Spain and is much in demand for its rarity and magical properties (i.e., the ability to cure impotence).

1614 The premiere of John Webster's *The Duchess of Malfi.*

Don Quixote

Financially challenged, romance-reading gent, La Mancha-based, seeks adventure. Has mare (Rosinante), salt-of-the-earth retainer (Sancho Panza), limitless credulity (takes windmills for giants); lacks partner ("Dulcinea del Toboso," DQ-restyled village lass). Mucho high jinks. Friend devises scheme to get DQ off chivalric jag. DQ croaks, mucho pathos. Cervantes' expansive, genially satirical portrait of Spanish society was an instant universal success, translated and parodied everywhere—despite which its author himself died in poverty.

Sir Philip Sidney, prime Elizabethan pin-up. Killed in action fighting the Spanish at Zutphen (1586).

Not to mention poor *Torquato Tasso* (1544–95), author of the Crusade epic *Jerusalem Delivered* (1581), a later devotee of the Estes whose persecution mania proved justified when they locked him up as insane.

But all this finespun poesy is—well—an acquired taste, as far as modern readers go. (Not to say that it's not worth acquiring: Spenser's "Mutabilitie" cantos, for example, are some of the most beautiful philosophical reflections in English.) While the period's prose writers of fiction can seem far more accessible, with their below-the-belt take on the dream worlds spun out by poets. The farting, belching, stuffing-yourself-silly fun of the giants Gargantua and Pantagruel, barging their iconoclastic way through mountains of spoof scholasticism and linguistic excess, outlives the targets of François Rabelais' satire (written in the 1520s and 30s).

Above all, it's in Spain that prose writing really takes off, with the racy lowlife of *Calisto and Melibea* (or *"La Celestina"*; Fernando de Rojas, 1502), and of the episodic picaresques (adventures concerning *picaros*, rogues). This is the form that would lead to realism's all-time riposte to romance and "poetry"; one of the most enduring of all fictions, Miguel de Cervantes' *Don Quixote* (1605–15; see box).

MEMO

For Rabelais, insist on Urquhart; the French genius found a Scottish translator of genius in the Royalist knight Sir Thomas U. (1611–60), working in exile after the Battle of Worcester.

1590 The first English paper mill is established at Dartford.

c. 1595 Narrow, heeled shoes become fashionable for European women. Previously, height has been achieved by the protective patten or the chopine, an ornamental stilt up to 18 inches high.

1596 Sir John Harington, courtier and translator, designs an early version of the water closet for Elizabeth I's palace at Richmond.

1599 The Globe playhouse is built, using timbers from an earlier theater. Destroyed by fire, rebuilt, and then demolished in 1644, it would not rise again until 1995.

1590~1610

All the World's a Stage
Will Shakespeare & Co.

Sebastien and Christopher clash in Act V of *Twelfth Night*.

Every now and then, drama descends from the stage to the page—play scripts become required reading. Most times, the two domains are distinct (that's why there's a Crash Course on Theater): who, apart from theater directors, wants to sit down and read Mystery plays, or Restoration comedies, or George Bernard Shaw? But, at certain periods, playwriting conspires with amazing poetry to produce something that seems more lifelike, more encompassing than any other form of reading: it happened in ancient Greece, it happened again in Elizabethan England.

In 1590s London, a bunch of young poets on the make—*Kit MARLOWE* (1564–93), *Ben JONSON* (1572–1637), and a certain *W. S.* (1564–1616)—decide their best chance lies in mounting the boards. Marlowe's a university graduate with a testosterone-charged imagination, exploring dreams of unlimited power in *Tamberlaine* and *Dr. Faustus;* he's gay, a rebel, a possible atheist, and is knifed to death at the age of 28 in a Deptford house. Jonson's a deeply educated moralist, but capable of some of the richest, rudest repartee (check *Bartholomew Fair*) and one of the most affecting short poems in the English language (on the death of his son, his "best piece of poetry").

As to Jonson's better-known friend: what can we say? His dad was a Catholic glovemaker. His son Hamnet died at age nine. He himself played the ghost in *Hamlet*. (Weird pattern of name echoes there.) He set trends (probably invented the "history play"), and also moved with them (following the more fashionable Beaumont & Fletcher in late plays like

> **MEMO**
> Jonson's lament for his child compares with one of the finest sequences in Polish poetry, the *Lamentations* of Jan Kochanowski (1534–80); see Seamus Heaney's translation.

1604 King James I publishes an antismoking pamphlet, saying it is "a custome lothsome to the eye, hatefull to the nose, harmefull to the braine, dangerous to the lungs."

1610 The "English bond" in brickwork is first used, alternating one row of headers with one of stretchers.

THE PLOT THICKENS

Meanwhile, in "Golden Age" Spain (1550–1650), the prodigious **Lope de Vega** *(1562–1635), often writing a play a day, totals some 1,500. Strangely, the quality sometimes matches the quantity—especially in his verse. Meanwhile* **Francisco de Quevedo** *(1580-1645), superb lyricist and sardonic satirist, offers the thought "Life begins in tears and shit."*

The Tempest). In effect, we know loads of trivia about him, but almost nothing self-revealing. He first makes his mark as an upstart getting on the nerves of a fellow scribbler, Robert Greene, in 1592. He's last heard of as a retired Stratford burgher,

dubiously involved in a scheme to enclose parishioners' smallholdings.

In between, *William SHAKESPEARE* (1564–1616) creates the English imagination: stretching out the language to its expressive fullness, exploring all that character, pathos, wit, sensual lyricism, and intellectual apprehension could mean in this tongue. He makes blank verse—unrhymed iambic pentameter, *di-dum-di-dum-di-dum-di-dum-di-dum*—a vehicle of infinite potential. And more than that, he shapes stories (remember, most of them weren't his own) into dramatic structures of a sturdiness that survives almost any translation.

Shakes & buddies, by Victorian John Faed: shocking stockings and a bit of ruff.

Bardfacts

"First Folio" (i.e., 1st collected edition, 1623) consists of 14 comedies, 10 histories, 12 tragedies, three or four partial-efforts, including the only surviving manuscript (sheet of *Sir Thomas More*). Longest: *Hamlet*. Shortest: *Macbeth*. 154 sonnets, 1–126 to nice young man ('Mr .W.H.'?), 127–152 to nasty woman. Three narrative poems (not so hot). Finest single-page critical portrait of Shakespeare: "Everything and Nothing," in *Labyrinths*, by Jorge Luis Borges (see p. 124).

1520 Henry VIII and François I have a three-week banquet in the Field of the Cloth of Gold near Calais; entertainment is so lavish that the French economy is crippled for the next ten years.

1581 The sedan chair is introduced into England.

1587 Mary, queen of Scots, is beheaded, on the orders of her sister Elizabeth I, for plotting against the English crown.

1520~1650
To God, to Bed
The Metaphysical Poets

God's in his heaven (or in that general direction), and all's right with the world (or not so wrong that the damage can't be paid for) … OR ELSE: God's right here. Behind you. With you. In you. (And everything you do is crucial.) This approximately was the clash of theologies that tore Europe apart in the upheavals of the 16th and 17th centuries. Among writers, the tension between accommodating worldliness and unsettling godliness would fall both sides of the Catholic/Protestant divide.

Burning for love: Nicholas Hilliard's miniature captures the spirit of lyric poetry.

Arcane ethos

Emblems were central to the spirit of "Metaphysical" writing. These could take the form of pictures matching the verse (as in Francis Quarles's *Emblems*, 1635) or of acrostics, or poems designed as pictures (both occur in Herbert's verse, prefiguring 20th-century "concrete poetry"). See the prose of Thomas Browne (i.e., *Urn Burial*, 1650s).

Secular love dominated most lyric writing, sure— for instance, the sonnets of Henry VIII's courtier Thomas Wyatt, or of the Venetian courtesan Gaspara Stampa, or, most significantly, of the leader of the French "Pléiade" poets, *Pierre DE RONSARD* (1524–85).

Yet in the contemporary poetry of Michelangelo (yes, *that* Michelangelo) and his friend Vittoria Colonna, there is already

the deep earnestness about God and Salvation that would gather force in the wake of Luther (himself no mean poet, in his hymns). It achieves its most concentrated, passionate form in the mystical songs of *San Juan DE LA CRUZ* (1542–91)—whose erotic spirituality earned him a halo.

England, too, had its Catholic poet saint— Robert Southwell, martyred in 1595—but, under the Church of England, the erotic and the spiritual occupy different

MEMO

The passion of Metaphysical lyrics is echoed by the first great poet of the "New World," the Mexican Sor Juana Ines de la Cruz (1652–95); she was also its first feminist.

1600 The cigarro (the Mayan for smoking is sik'ar) is introduced to Europe. Paper-wrapped cigarettes are an invention of Seville beggars, using tobacco from cigar-butts.

1615 Cornelius von Drebbel builds a submarine of wood and leather and rows it underwater from Westminster to Greenwich.

1640 John Evelyn (1620–1706) starts keeping a diary. When published in 1818, it proves to be of great historical interest.

compartments. First *John DONNE* (1572–1631) spends his youth bed-hopping around all the classiest four-posters in London—or making out that he has, at least, in the furiously macho, braggadoccio "Elegies" and the full-of-heart-but-oh-so-smart "Songs and Sonnets." Then—some time after the religious questioning recorded in his great "Third Satire"—he takes orders, and directs his energies into bargaining with the Almighty as Dean of St. Pauls. Either way, he's the most disruptively intelligent, the most streetwise and—even across four centuries—the most definitively modern of English poets.

His complex intellectual conceits are what Dryden, later, would call "Metaphysical" poetry; a comparable convolution can be found in the contemporary Spanish of *Luis DE GÓNGORA* (1561–1627) and in the Italian of *Giambattista MARINO* (1569–1625).

But the style needn't lead to intense brow-knotting; if you want *positive*, gracefully intelligent religious verse, turn to the The Temple (1633)

THE PLOT THICKENS

"Metaphysical," but outside the on-your-knees brigade; personally opaque; yet unequivocally, commandingly excellent: **Andrew Marvell** *(1621–78), MP for Hull. Sensualist of "The Garden"; tough-minded politico of "An Horatian Ode upon Cromwell's Return from Ireland"; satirist attacking corruption in "Last Instructions to a Painter"; and author of the greatest panties-off message in English poetry, "To His Coy Mistress."*

by the priest *George HERBERT* (1593–1633) or to the shimmeringly fresh mystical visions of his successors—*Silex Scintillans* (1650) by *Henry VAUGHAN* (1621–95) and *Centuries of Meditation* by *Thomas TRAHERNE* (1637–74).

Mean 'n' moody charisma, c. 1595: John Donne poses for Anon. with a bunch of raw sausages.

1630 An Amsterdam pearl merchant buys 24 miles by 48 miles of land on the west of the Hudson River. He pays the Indians "certain quantities of duffels, axes, knives and wampum."

1640 *The Bay Psalm Book*, the first American book, is published in Cambridge, Massachusetts. It will be in use until 1773.

1647 The first-known advertisements appear in *Perfect Occurrences of Every Day*.

1630 ~ 1670

The Milton Problem
Radical Puritans

John MILTON (1608–74) is like Dante Alighieri in this: he's a hard man, of tough, radical religious views, with vast poetical capabilities and an absolutely enormous literary ambition to match. "Things unattempted yet in prose or verse … to justify the ways of God to Man," that's what the preamble to Paradise Lost *(1667) immodestly aims at. Milton's not like Dante in this: half the world hates him.* Paradise Lost *has got to be the most controversial great poem ever written—continuing to get on people's nerves after more than three centuries. Why is this?*

Milton as a young man, before he lost his sight; painted by Samuel Cooper.

Milton continued
"God is alive and well, and working on a less ambitious project." Much in the spirit of the old college graffiti chestnut, Milton went on from *Paradise Lost* to a smaller-scale, rather drab follow-up, *Paradise Regained* (re Christ's temptation), and the defiant, deeply personal *Samson Agonistes* (both 1671), a verse drama about the glorious death of the Old Testament hero modeled on Greek tragedy.

H ere at *Crash Course*, we don't have any problems. We think the stylistic range that Milton perfected through his youthful stuff—the turn from pastoral sweetness to prophetic anger in the beautiful elegy *Lycidas*, on a drowned friend, and the extraordinary moral gravity of his sonnets—serves him well when he goes on to write up heaven and hell. We think that if he wants to be England's Virgil, aping the structure of the *Æneid* in a massively extended paraphrase of the first four chapters of

Milton's legacy
In Germany, Gottlieb Klopstock's four-book poem, *Der Messias* (1748–73), can be seen as an attempt to do for the Redemption what Milton had done for the Fall.

Genesis, taking in all that went before (i.e., the war in heaven between God and Satan), and, in prophecy, all that would come after (right down to the problems Milton's Puritan party was having in 17th-century England), well, he's a lot less boring than his model.

We love the sheer generosity of his imagination, dreaming up and recreating every detail of the natural and the supernatural world—down to the creation of the animals, bursting out of bumps in the soil.

1650 All continents except Antarctica are known to Europe.

1650 Tea is first drunk in England; the first coffee house opens in Oxford.

1670 Actress Nell Gwynn, who began her career selling oranges in the theater, becomes the mistress of King Charles II.

THE PLOT THICKENS

The other great testament to the radical thought of Puritan England is The Pilgrim's Progress *(1678), written (partly in Bedford Prison) by the Dissenter* **John Bunyan**: *that rare thing, a truly popular religious allegory.* **John Wesley** *(1703–91) was part of a later revival of popular piety.*

But boy, the flak sure keeps on coming. Milton misunderstands women! ("O Eve, in evil hour …" Adam accuses: yes, it's true. Milton's pretty bad here.) Milton misunderstands the English language! (This one comes from Samuel Addison and Dr. Johnson, claiming he's squeezing English into Latin styles of diction, strangling native idioms and, in leaving his epic unrhymed, abandoning native versification.) Milton misunderstands himself! (Cue William Blake, subversively suggesting that the reason Satan, not God, seems the hero of the poem is that "Milton was a true poet, and of the devil's party without knowing it.") Milton misunderstands God! (Even atheist critics like William Empson reproach him for this.)

These are the kinds of problem you run up against if you try something too conceptually ambitious, particularly in England. People begin to take you as seriously as you take yourself, and start checking your work against reality … Crazy! it's only a poem! (Or is it? Perhaps poems change reality by making people do things? I'll leave you to decide.)

Milton's hero? Satan rousing the rebel angels in a 1688 illustration to *P. L.*

1664 Jean-Baptiste Lully (1632–87), the founder of French opera, composes music for Molière's ballets.

1680 The dodo, a stout, flightless bird found on the Mascarene Islands, becomes extinct after having been relentlessly pursued for food and feathers.

1690 Wallpaper is invented; "Edward Butting … maketh … a sort of paper in imitation of Irish stitch … Flock work, Wainscot, Marble, Damask, Turkey work etc."

1 6 6 0 ~ 1 7 3 0

Let's Be Reasonable
French Classicism

1648: the Peace of Westphalia closes 130 years of religious conflict in Europe. 1660: the English Revolution collapses, and King Charles II takes up the throne. Major cultural pressure-drop. Big change of project. New head honcho for literature …

Monsieur Jourdain in *Le Bourgeois Gentilhomme.*

> *Let Puritan dissension fade from sight,*
> *By smooth and smirking Couplets put to flight.*
> *O pleasant days! O happy ruling class!*
> *For Dryden longs to kiss the Royal ass.*

Yes, well, enough of the superslick *John Dryden* (1631–1700), taking his cue in London from the more intellectually vital writers of Paris. From the mid 17th century, French culture led Europe on all fronts, with a commanding energy that was in fact largely devoted to self-control. The apostle of this restraint, in literature, had been *François Malherbe* (1556–1628), insisting on good poetic form and rational sense. His precepts helped shape the grand, declamatory verse of the dramatist *Pierre Corneille* (1606–84), and through him, that of the comedian *Molière* (1622–73) and the tragedian *Jean Racine* (1639–99).

Wigs, Whigs, coffeepots, and conversation. A London coffeehouse c.1705. Note printed matter on the tables: the growth of lit-crit culture.

1697 Champion of contemporary French writers, poet, and critic Charles Perrault (1628–1703) will be best remembered for his *Contes de ma mère l'Oye* (Tales of Mother Goose).

1710 British astronomer Edmond Halley, comparing star positions with those listed by Ptolemy, discovers the independent motion of the stars.

1714 Henry Mill patents "an artificial machine or method for impressing or transcribing of letters singly or progressively"—but no typewriter emerges yet.

The pygmy Pope, portrayed with panache by Sir Godfrey Kneller.

Molière is almost as central to French literature as Shakespeare is to English: creating, through resoundingly durable caricatures like *Le Bourgeois Gentilhomme* (1660) or *Tartuffe* (1664), a whole way of seeing individuals within their social context—setting them up within it and laughing at them, but in a generous spirit. Racine, by contrast, sets individuals on trajectories of extreme, desperate passion, and slams them up hard against the constraints of the social order—as in the tragedy of *Phèdre*'s incestuous love for her son-in-law Hippolyte (1677).

These dramatists, along with lesser versifiers like *Jean DE LA FONTAINE* (1621–95), writer of the *Fables*, and the character-sketch writer *Jean DE LA BRUYÈRE* (1645–96), together make up a "French classicism" whose principles would be codified by *Nicolas BOILEAU* (1636–1711). The advocacy of taste, reason, and clarity in Boileau's *Art poétique* feeds back onto a later generation of "Augustan" writers across the water—above all *Alexander POPE* (1688–1744) and his friend in Dublin, *Jonathan SWIFT* (1667–1745). Pope is a four-foot-six literary phenomenon, dazzlingly witty, adept, and viciously vituperative; Swift, passionate and honorable yet sardonic and dark in his dealings with politicians, with women, in fact with the whole human race. The weird thing about these would-be successors to Virgil and Horace is that their writing really comes alive, not so much in praise of classical ideals (i.e., Pope's *An Essay on Man*, 1733–34) as in deranged, obsessive invective against their adversaries (Pope's *The Dunciad*, 1728–43, Swift's uproariously bizarre *A Tale of a Tub*, 1704). (You want *Gulliver's Travels*? See p. 37.)

> **MEMO**
>
> The wittiest verse of the English Restoration comes from the libertine Earl of Rochester (1647–80)—"The Maimed Debauchee" as he styled himself in one of his more printable pieces.

Alexandrines

France's equivalent to the "heroic couplet" of Dryden and Pope was the coupleted "alexandrine"—i.e., a line of six feet, defined, as with classical verse, by vowel-quantity rather than stress. (The lighter stresses of French, as opposed to English, lie behind the awfulness of all French rock music.)

1697 Peter the Great, Tsar of Russia, using the name Peter Michailoff, works in the dockyards of Saarden, in Holland, and Deptford, in London.

1709 Alexander Selkirk, marooned on the Island of Juan Fernandez, is rescued; his account, published in 1713, will inspire Defoe's *Robinson Crusoe.*

1710 The Statute of Anne, the first copyright law, recognizes authors' rights and specifies a limited term of protection after which works will enter the public domain.

1670~1750

Character Building
Early Novels

Lots of literary historians will tell you that "the novel"—you know, that thing where rounded characters, complex social situations, and even more complex psychological experiences are put into life-size prose— only became possible in 18th-century Europe. Garbage. Every part of that definition is fulfilled by the Tale of Genji, *written by a lady of the Japanese court—pseudonym Murasaki Shibiku—just after the year 1000. The trouble is, Europe had to wait a long time to catch up with this vast, witty, subtly nuanced, and assured prose performance (in fact, no Japanese came near it either).*

A contemporary engraving of Defoe's Robinson Crusoe.

It was another high-society lady who became the first exponent of this type of fiction in France. *Mme. DE LA FAYETTE* (1634–93) reads pretty tamely now; for its time, however, *La Princesse de Clèves* (1678) opened up new ways to display the intimate emotions of a love triangle. But the idea took a while to catch on. Romance and Spanish picaresque were still the ways to do storytelling—as in Aphra Behn's anti-colonialist *Oroonoko* (1688) or the episodic lowlife of Johannes Grimmelshausen's *Simplicissimus* (1669). The brusque, factual prose of *Daniel DEFOE* (?1660–1731) in *Robinson Crusoe* (1719)—the original "desert island" myth—builds on models like these. In *Moll Flanders* (1722), however, superhack Defoe (560-odd publications!) makes "character"—the way a certain psychology interacts with a certain society—a factor in

1728 *The Beggar's Opera* is first performed—making Gay (the author) rich and Rich (the producer) gay.

1735 William Hogarth publishes a series of satirical engravings entitled *A Rake's Progress*, the story of a young man's corruption and decline.

1736 India rubber is first brought to England; by 1744, it will be widely used.

Gulliver's Travels

Totally *against* the realistic trend: the all-encompassing satire of Swift's *Gulliver's Travels* (1726). Lemuel G. visits (1) Lilliput's midgets—mocking small-minded religion; (2) Brobdingnag's giants—who look dimly on European civilization; (3) the deranged scientific speculators of Laputa; (4) the Houyhnhnms, noble horses served by vile "Yahoos"—in other words, *us*.

The Abbé Prévost amuses a Parisienne at her levée with his *Manon Lescaut*.

the unrolling adventures of a highly successful whore. Compare the Abbé Prévost's combination, in *Manon Lescaut* (1731), of intense personal emotions with wild events on far-off shores. The focus starts to swing from *What happened next?* to *How did they feel about it?*

It's a far-reaching shift—capped by the remarkable decision of Samuel Richardson, a 50-year-old London printer, to pen his first novel in 1740 in "epistolary" form—i.e., as a correspondence. The vastly successful *Pamela* and its vast successor *Clarissa* (1749)—both tales of seduction—will open up, for

European readers, whole new swathes of moral nuance, scruple, and "sentiment."

In this sense, *Henry FIELDING* (1707–54), mocking Richardson with the spoof *Shamela* (developed into *Joseph Andrews*, 1742), is going against the trend, opting for the Spanish model of Cervantes (as would his follower *Tobias SMOLLETT*, 1721–71). But Fielding's bluff, full-hearted, naturalistic—OK, somewhat rosy-tinged—picture of contemporary country life in *Tom Jones* (1749) would be just as important as Richardson's fine feelings in setting standards for future English fiction.

Moral support

Fielding was a friend and ally of the painter Hogarth, describing him as a "Comic History-Painter." In fact Hogarth's pictures, each unfolding a complex moralizing plot, can be seen as visual equivalents to Fielding's novels.

1727 House rats appear in Europe, having crossed the continent from eastern Siberia.

1752 Benjamin Franklin demonstrates lightning to be electricity.

1754 Scotland's Royal and Ancient Golf Course is founded in St. Andrews.

1720s~1770s

Critical Mass

Voltaire and Dr. Johnson

"Criticism is easy, art is difficult"—thus wrote Philippe Destouches in 1732. Or, as Kenneth Tynan would later put it, "A critic is a man who knows the way but can't drive the car." We all despise them; most of us read them from time to time; some of us—horrors!—are them. But no one really wants a criticocracy—a culture so dominated by criticism that creativity is effectively stifled.

That, though, is just about what you got in mid-18th century Europe. In the wake of the "classical" rule making of Boileau, Pope, *et al.* (see pp. 34–5), poetry was squeezed into a very narrow corner, imaginatively. A corner, it's true, from which there issued some of the great "Quite Nice" poems of English literature, such as James Thomson's *The Seasons* (1730) or Thomas Gray's *Elegy Written in a Country Churchyard* (1750). But the central figures in both the French and English inkworlds were dogmatic finger-waggers. Both used fiction, but as a form of criticism by other means. And each would deeply affect his national culture—but in quite different directions.

From the 1720s, *François-Marie Arouet* (1694–1778), a.k.a. Voltaire, was the big noise in Paris—even though he was banned from that town by the king for much of his working life. Scribbling in foreign courts, or in the country retreat of Ferney, he dashed off the brilliantly sprightly satire on philosophic optimism, *Candide* (1759), among a huge assortment of screeds philosophical, critical, and political. What Voltaire, along with the likewise polymathic Denis Diderot, was urging forward was a liberal, open-minded culture, free of religious hypocrisy—he

French letters

The *ancien régime* culture Voltaire was savaging gets its most incisive—and cynical—portrayal in the epistolary novel of Choderlos de Laclos, *Les Liaisons Dangéreuses* (1782).

1761 Thomas Arne's *Judith* is performed, the first oratorio in England t require female singers.

1762 Engraver and mapmaker John Spilsbury pastes maps onto wood then cuts them up to make the first jigsaws; educational toys for children.

1774 The Earl of Chesterfield's *Letters* are published; according to Dr. Johnson, "they teach the morals of a whore and the manners of a dancing-master."

Joshua Reynolds' uncompromising portrait of Johnson.

MEMO

Boswell may have been Johnson's sidekick, but he certainly had a life of his own: read about it in his hilariously self-dramatizing *London Journal* (1762–63).

(1759)—but chiefly directs his lugubrious energies to gathering up the national language and literature. The *Dictionary* (1754); his *Preface to Shakespeare* (1765); and his *Lives of the Poets* (1781) solidify Englishness in magisterial prose. Johnson's profoundly stoic, unillusioned but humorous temper shows through above all in the records his Scottish friend James Boswell makes of their conversations. It is English conservatism at its most plausible, and it would affect the culture permanently.

thought he saw such a thing in England. When he died in 1778—fêted on a return to Paris—he had laid the intellectual foundations of the French Revolution.

In England, meanwhile, *Samuel Johnson* (1709–84), Doctor of Letters, goes in for philosophic satire in *Rasselas*

THE PLOT THICKENS

"Nothing odd will do for long." That was Johnson's comment on Tristram Shandy, *the most effervescent, anarchic ripping-up of everything that could be done with the book format ever.* **Laurence Sterne's** *nine-volume, generously characterized, deliriously digressioned memoir of the first five years of the life of T. S. reads as immediately as it did in the 1760s, giving the lie to the dour Doctor.*

The cult of Voltaire: a Parisian salon gets together to read one of his tragedies in 1755, gathered beneath a bust of the impish pundit.

1770 The visiting card is introduced in England.

1776 Edward Gibbon publishes volume one of his massive *History of the Decline and Fall of the Roman Empire*; it will not be completed until 1788.

1778 Viennese physician Franz Anton Mesmer first practices mesmerism in Paris.

1781 Using a 7-foot reflecting telescope, Sir Frederick William Herschel (1738–1822) discovers the planet Uranus.

1770~1800

Folk of Genius

Extravagant Visionaries

The modishly absurd Sir Brooke Boothby squashes a volume of Rousseau; painting by Joseph Wright of Derby.

DRANG! O.K., "Sturm und Drang," if you insist: it just sounds more impactful that way. Suddenly, in the 1770s, there's an explosion of literary production: scores of young scribblers all over Germany penning wild, extravagantly emotional, over-the-top dramas of "Storm and Stress." Most of this stuff, it's true, is forgettable; but not the plays and poems of Friedrich SCHILLER (1759–1805), nor the work of his older friend Johann Wolfgang VON GOETHE (1749–1832). The latter's Sorrows of Young Werther—a preposterous but winning effusion about unlucky love, ending in suicide—was Europe's most popular novel in its day, Napoleon's favorite bedside read.

W here were these guys coming from? Firstly, they had both been reading the works of *Jean-Jacques ROUSSEAU* (1712–78)—philosophic scourge of corrupt civilization, advocate of natural simplicity and sentiment, itinerant guru, friend (then enemy) of Voltaire, Diderot, and almost everyone he met—

author, moreover, of the lovesick and lachrymose, semiautobiographical *La Nouvelle Héloïse* (1761). Secondly, their friend *Johann HERDER* (1744–1803) pointed the way forward in focusing on folk traditions in culture. Forget all that phony classicism; get back to genuine feeling through ballads, sagas, Northern myths, "roots" stuff as we'd say now. Goethe *et al.* reckoned they'd found the real thing in "the Celtic Homer"—"Ossian." They were dead wrong: "Ossian" was an epic fraud, concocted in the 1760s by the Gaelic scholar James Macpherson.

Cheating Tom
Another fashionable fraud: the "15th-century" poems of "Thomas Rowley," a.k.a. Bristol teenager Thomas Chatterton (1752–70), who killed himself in a London garret at age 18. Subsequently a hero to Wordsworth and Keats.

1791 Mozart writes his *Zauberflöte, La Clemenza di Tito, Fantasia in F,* and, on his deathbed, his *Requiem;* he is buried in an unmarked pauper's grave.

1800 Wife-beater and nagging wife; characters from the Italian *Commedia dell'Arte* metamorphose into the very British Punch and Judy puppet show.

Goethe, personally, moved on. He helped run the Duchy of Weimar; he involved himself in botany and optical theory; in 1786 he toured Italy, where he came to a new reconciliation with the idea of "classicism." His later novel, *Elective Affinities* (1809), is far more emotionally sophisticated than *Werther*. He returned repeatedly, through his long career, to the fictional life of *Wilhelm Meister*—the original *Bildungsroman*, or novel of personal development—and to the lofty cosmic allegories of the poem *Faust*. Goethe's prodigious (and benevolent) energies sprawled into myriad different forms—there is no figure like him in English culture.

One of the most extraordinary figures that English culture does possess was sidelined into obscurity throughout his working life in London. Once dismissed as insane, *William BLAKE* (1757–1827) is now recognized, not only as the writer of some of England's most powerful visionary lyrics, and as an artist of genius, but also as the most politically acute member of its radical, religiously dissenting Awkward Squad. Go from the *Songs of Innocence*

and of *Experience* (1789, 1794) to the challenge and fire of *The Marriage of Heaven & Hell* (1790–93). If really bold: go to the allegorical complexities and biblical grandeur of the "prophetic books": *Vala, or the Four Zoas* (1797), *Milton* (1808), and *Jerusalem* (1820).

Scots bard
The real thing: Robert Burns (1759–96) possessed by birthright all the "folk" qualities that critics like Herder valued—a sure feel for the landscape of his native Lowlands and for its songs, stories, and people; an infectious emotional heat, and a radical, cut-the-bullshit common touch. He also possessed no money, and an uncommon thirst. Result: Scotland's national poet. Even if not Scottish, read *Tam o'Shanter* (1791).

MEMO
Blake is less well known as a hilariously caustic critic and satirist. His commentaries on his artistic enemies (notably Sir Joshua Reynolds) are infectiously, irresistibly irate.

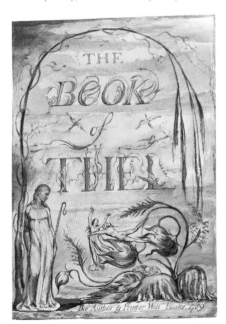

A hand-colored frontispiece by "The Author & Printer Willm. Blake, 1789" for *The Book of Thel*, an early mystical publication.

1791-92 Thomas Paine, revolutionary, publishes *The Rights of Man.*

1797 Jacques Garnerin makes the first parachute drop from a balloon; his parachute, derived from the parasol, oscillates wildly—the first case of airsickness?

1800 Italian physicist Alessandro Volta invents the first electric battery.

1790~1815

Guillotines and Country Cottages
Wordsworth, Coleridge, and Austen

Throughout Europe, the 18th century draws to a close excitingly, alarmingly, giddily. Anything seems possible in the light of the French Revolution. Where is the writer who will speak for these stirring times?

Wordsworth (elderly sheep phase), portrayed with wife in early Victorian reverence.

With his neck on the guillotine. *André Chénier* (1762–94), the brightest poet of his day in France, falls foul of Robespierre—as a moderate—and has time to pen little more than the jailbound, defiant *Iambes.* Meanwhile, passing through revolutionary Paris in 1791—"Bliss was it in that dawn to be alive!"—comes a young English poet with a loftier sense of mission than any since Milton. Nature had confided her imaginative truths to *William Wordsworth* (1770–1850)—or so he believed—and he arrives at a new, plainspoken poetic diction in which to convey them to the world at large. It was a sort of literary revolution. Writing his great *Ode on Intimations of Immortality*, or recounting his Lakeland child-hood in the autobiographic *The Prelude*, Wordsworth makes poetry into a new vehicle for everyone's personal experience, through his unselfconscious earnestness and unadorned clarity.

Ah, but: "Two voices hast thou, Wordsworth:"—let's slightly misquote J. K. Stephen—"one is of the deep ... The other, the bleating of an old half-witted sheep." The youth so memorably startled by the daffodils turns into a reactionary plodder come middle age, a monument to wordy, worthy tedium. Why do poets fizzle out?

Fanny Burney

Austen's predecessor: Fanny Burney (1752–1840), friend of Dr. Johnson, lady-in-waiting at court; author of *Evelina* (1778), the first English novel to make the everyday, vulgar embarrassments of an average girl the stuff of comedy.

1803 The Lyceum theater in London is experimentally lit by gas.

1807 The slave trade is abolished in Jamaica and on board British ships.

1812–15 The Brothers Grimm publish their *Fairy Tales*, a collection of German folktales drawn directly from folk sources.

Wordsworth's collaborator in the *Lyrical Ballads* of 1798, Samuel TAYLOR COLERIDGE (1772–1834), almost made that question his principal theme. Having turned out the unforgettable phantasmagoria of *The Rime of the Ancient Mariner*, he turned to the fine art of talent-wasting—the first of the great failures. He did it in style: just think how boring *Kubla Khan* might have become if not for the famous interruption of S.T.C.'s drugged reverie by a "person from Porlock."

Far removed from all visions and revolutions, yet sharing the same era: "three or four families in a country village," the theme worked up in supremely poised, razor-sharp prose by *Jane AUSTEN* (1775–1817). Scribbling in her corner of a Hampshire vicarage parlor, keeping her sights on her familiar world, she brings a newly *classical* attitude to prose fiction—formal composure, a conservative and ironic eye, "the most thorough knowledge of human nature ... conveyed to the world in the best chosen language." She became a minor cult in the 19th century; then rose to the status of major cultural monument in the 20th.

Jane Austen. A Victorian print adapted from a likeness by her sister Cassandra.

THE PLOT THICKENS

Austen's favorite poet, Wordsworth's peer in plainspokenness: **George Crabbe** *(1754–1832), baleful realist of Suffolk's rural miseries. Crabbe's forebear in poetic pessimism:* **William Cowper** *(1731–1800), a certified depressive with a tender, self-deprecating humor. Both promote a sensitivity to nature and a social conscience that would flavor the whole idea of "literary culture" in England. Literary culture, during the Industrial Revolution, was increasingly widely disseminated through the new "circulating libraries." The form that would be most promoted as a result of this new mass market was the novel.*

Before Scott

Castle Rackrent (1800) by Maria Edgeworth (1768–1849) is the first real historical novel in English. It is a racy, rambunctious narrative of recklessly improvident aristos in her native Ireland.

Here at *Crash Course*, we recognize the strength and roundedness of her creations; but, as a cultural model, we say it's time her snide, staid, quasi-incestuous fictional setup was relegated to obscurity.

1800 There are estimated to be five billion passenger pigeons in North America. In the Northwest territories they use them as a low-cost food source.

1809 Napoleon Bonaparte has his marriage to Josephine annulled because of her infertility.

1812 Surgeon Baron Dominique Jean Larrey performs 200 amputations in the 24 hours following the Battle of Borodino.

1800~1825

Romantic Disasters
Odes and Early Deaths

Keats, improving on Shakespeare in a Hampstead drawing room, c. 1819.

Despairingly, he lifts his gaze to the night skies. He yearns to recapture some lost vision—of ethereal feminine beauty, of some far-off age where all are bound in mystic harmony. He sighs, and scrawls some rhymes. He reaches for the laudanum. He could do with a good haircut, his clothing is threadbare, and, one way or another, he will soon be pushing up daisies. Ahh! the Romantic poet … the figure around which August and Friedrich Schlegel, Ludwig Tieck, and Friedrich von Hardenburg started to coin their philosophy of "Romanticism," c.1800. A man of world-transcending "genius," this figure—an imagination soaring beyond the cramping rules of "classicism"; a soul straining for the spiritual and the infinite, yet ironically bound by the limitations of flesh and language.

Lamentably

A late Romantic tragedy: that of John Clare (1793–1864). His verse, with its intimate knowledge of the Northamptonshire countryside reflecting his peasant roots, was briefly popular in the 1820s. When it passed from vogue he was left adrift: he entered an insane asylum in 1837, to spend 30 years writing in isolation, sometimes with great poignancy, of his predicament.

A bit of a disaster area, in other words. Watch them fall down: F. von H., a.k.a. "Novalis," dies of TB at 39, after writing the beautiful *Hymns to the Night* mourning the death of his 16-year-old fiancée. Friedrich Hölderlin, pursuing his chokingly intense visions of ancient Greece, is burnt out by insanity a year later,

although he will witlessly survive another thirty-four. Heinrich von Kleist—less Romantic poet than chillingly powerful master of the "novella," the long short story—culminates his restless career in a suicide pact. Coleridge (see p. 43), shamelessly plagiarizing the German theorists, becomes an opium-sodden wreck—as does the journalist Thomas De Quincey, who would brilliantly describe the addiction in prose.

The next rising stars of Eng Lit fall into

1819 The largest known hearing aid is King John VI of Portugal's "acoustic throne"; a lion's mouth captures the sound and resonators convey it to the royal ear.

1822 French scholar Jean François Champollion deciphers the hieroglyphics of the Rosetta Stone.

1825 Scottish explorer Alexander Gordon Laing becomes the first European to go to Timbuktu.

this pattern also. Romanticism's tricky fellow: the politically extreme, personally impossible *Percy Bysshe SHELLEY* (1792–1822), aristo thrown out of Oxford for atheism, plunging into idealistic projects and ménages-à-trois—and out of them as fast—flees England for Italy, where he drowns off Lerici. Somehow, he manages beforehand to produce a body of verse of extraordinary artistic and intellectual command (besides many reams of rant). And Romanticism's all-time good guy: *John KEATS* (1795–1821), hostler's son, mocked-at Cockney shortass, luckless lover of the lucklessly named Fanny Brawne, scribbles away against the stopwatch of his own consumption, rapaciously extending the reach of his sensuous intelligence, pacing himself against Shakespeare, to produce—in his "Odes"—the nearest approach by another writer to the unified sensibility of England's greatest poet.

THE PLOT THICKENS

Another disaster area: the body of **Giacomo Leopardi** *(1798–1837). Hunchbacked, half-blind, half-deaf, stuck moreover in an isolated manorial library in the dreariest backwoods of an Italy that had itself become a cultural backwater. Not the kind of experience that leads to sunny joie-de-vivre? No, it certainly wasn't: the theme of Leopardi's poetry is total pessimism, total disillusionment. Yet, strangely, the verse itself is radiantly clear, deeply sympathetic, and intelligent, plangently beautiful in its evocations of the Italian countryside. Worth learning Italian for.*

The funeral of Shelley: fetched from the Tyrrhenian Sea, his body burns as his buddy Byron (white-scarfed) looks on. By Louis Forain, 1889.

1812 The ruins of Petra, ancient Arab capital, are identified by Jean Louis Burckhardt, doyen of Middle East explorers.

1812 An "elastic round hat" is advertised; a steel spring inside the crown allows the fabric to be compressed and the hat collapsed.

1813 Uncle Sam, the symbol of the United States, is used for the first time.

1810~1840

National Heroes
Byron and Pushkin

Lord Byron, did I hear you say? Isn't he right smack at the heart of this business called "Romanticism?" You're right, he is, but in that cult of the individual, what he wrote mattered less than what he was. Mr. "Mad, Bad, and Dangerous to Know"; the man who "woke up to find himself famous" all over London on the publication of Childe Harolde's Pilgrimage *(1812); the darkly handsome clubfoot who swam the Hellespont; the lover who moved from adulteries to incest (with his half-sister Augusta); the liberal moved to sacrifice his life for the liberty of Greece (or at any rate to catch a fatal fever on its soil)—this is the central image of Romanticism, its selling point.*

Lord Byron Reposing in the House of a Fisherman Having Swum the Hellespont by Sir William Allen. What more can we say?

MEMO

It was a longstanding problem for Russians to demonstrate to foreigners that their Pushkin was a world-beating poet, because every translation left him sounding flat. This problem was effectively solved when Charles Johnston's brilliant version of *Eugene Onegin* came out in 1978. Read it and relish.

The actual literary remains are a motley set. Some seductive lyrics; a lot of picturesque, emotion-charged narrative (including *Harolde*); but, at its best, Byron's writing is on an almost *anti*-Romantic tangent.

Don Juan (1819–24) is a rolling narrative dominated by hilariously debunking satire—much of it directed at the likes of Wordsworth, and looking back for its model to Pope's verse. But think about Byron's death in the fight for Greek independence from Turkey. In Europe after Napoleon's defeat, Romanticism—with its quest for individuality of spirit, and for "folk values"—led partly toward liberalism; more toward *nationalism*. It followed that every nation needed to find

1830 Edwin Budding patents a "machine for cropping or shearing the vegetable surface of lawns, grass plots, and pleasure-gardens"—the lawnmower.

1831 Frédéric Chopin, Polish composer, moves to Paris. After his stormy liaison with George Sand and early death, he comes to represent the archetypal Romantic artist.

1840 Afternoon tea is introduced by Anna, duchess of Bedford.

its own distinctive poetic voice. This was the point when ballad-collecting took off, when the brothers Grimm gathered their grisly tales, when the ancient myths of Finland were written down as the *Kalevala* (1822). The time when *Adam MICKIEWICZ* (1798–1855) gave voice to Polishness in the fervently patriotic epic *Pan Tadeusz* (1834), and when the uplifting songs of *Sándor PETŐFI* (1823–56?) earned him the comparative status of "the Robert Burns of Hungary."

Which brings us to a greater literary artist than Byron: *Aleksandr PUSHKIN* (1799–1837), the one writer all Russians agree in revering, the cornerstone of their culture. As with Byron, the life's a part of the deal: the ancestry from an African slave, the death in a duel. But it's the mobility and tenderness of Pushkin's voice, and the freshness of his vision, that makes

THE PLOT THICKENS

Liberty, irony, pathos: the key values of Byron's poetry reappear in the lyrics of **Heinrich Heine** *(1797–1856), the German Jewish writer whose yearning sentimentality would be a cue for many of the 19th century's favorite Lieder, and whose brilliantly sardonic, irreverent take on Germany's political and intellectual authorities lives on in his prose writings.*

him grab the Russian heart. He takes on foreign models—Byron and other Romantic sources in his lyrics, Shakespeare in his drama *Boris Godunov*—and transmutes them, above all in the magnificent verse novel *Eugene Onegin* (1831). In *The Bronze Horseman* (1833) he creates a resounding central myth for the great city of St. Petersburg.

Flamboyant, witty, and radical, Pushkin recites before the court's crusty reactionaries. As imagined by Russian historical realist Ilya Repin.

1816 The British Museum buys the Elgin marbles, smuggled from Greece by Lord Elgin.

1818 Thomas Bowdler publishes his *Family Shakespeare*, from which he attempts to exclude all "profaneness or obscenity"; hence, to "bowdlerize" or expurgate.

1823 Charles Macintosh patents the waterproof fabric from which raincoats are to be made.

1829 Sir Robert Peel's Metropolitan Police Act is passed, reorganizing and reforming the capital's police force; the London "Bobby" or "Peeler" emerges.

1810-1845

Offering Up History
Popular Novels

James Fenimore Cooper. *(See below.)*

Walter SCOTT *(1771–1832), a lawyer with ambitions as a social grandee, discovers in 1812 that Lord Byron—like him, Scottish, club-footed, and possessed of awesome verbal facility—has cornered his market. No one is buying his verse any more. He thinks he'll try his hand at prose. Result:* Waverley, *gripping tale of the Jacobite Rebellion of 1745, issued anonymously in 1814. Wild success, talk of the town (literature is becoming more and more a publicity phenomenon, thanks to the growth of the press).*

Encouraged, Scott expands the historical novel market with *The Heart of Midlothian*, *Ivanhoe*, and much, much more. Meanwhile, he buys into his publishers; builds a big house as a monument to Scottishness; climaxes his career by staging the reception of King George IV in Edinburgh in 1822, hailed by massed clans in tartan; overreaches himself financially; crashes (1826). The rest of his life is spent furiously writing his way out of debt. When he expires, exhausted, in 1832, he has not only created a nine-tenths phony Scottish heritage industry, he has also changed the shape of literature. The Scott phenomenon (which is complicated by the fact that, for all his fusty garrulity, this odious timeserver lives on as a

writer with vast imaginative gifts) is echoed not only in Europe but in the U.S. James Fenimore COOPER (1789–1851) was performing a comparable myth-making operation on the early frontiersmen of the West, most famously in *The Last of the Mohicans* (1826), set back in colonial times, and in *The Deerslayer* (1841), introducing the character of Natty Bumppo. History was becoming *chewier*: you didn't just set your tale in the past to skirt overtly topical reference (as had long been the custom), you lingered over the flavor of the bygone. Alessandro Manzoni's *The Betrothed* (1825–42), set in the Spanish-ruled Italy of the 1640s, is not only a knock at the Austrian-ruled Italy of Manzoni's day but a massive and loving act of

French history
Scott hits Paris: poet Alfred de Vigny gets historical in the novel *Cinq-Mars* (1826), based on a conspiracy against Cardinal Richelieu, doing over the 17th century for France as Scott had done for Scotland.

1830 A London merchant invents the commercial tin canister, as a means of preserving food. The tin bears the instruction, "Cut round on the top with a chisel and hammer."

1840 Mikhail Lermontov, Russian romantic poet, publishes his prose masterpiece *A Hero of Our Time.* He will be killed in a duel in 1841.

reconstruction, sympathizing with the lives of the poor in past times. (It is also the novel that did most to unite modern Italian national consciousness.)

The novel expands exponentially from this stage. While it reaches out for history and politics, it also delves within to explore psychology, as in Benjamin Constant's analysis of love in *Adolphe* (1816), or does both, as in the great novels of "Stendhal" (a.k.a. *Henri BEYLE,* 1783–1842). Stendhal, a cultured veteran of Napoleon's wars, skeptical yet passionate, romantic yet analytical, gives shape to his angular impulses in *Le Rouge et le noir* (1831), a richly imagined tale of a contemporary social climber, and in the participant's vision of the Battle of Waterloo that heads *La Chartreuse de Parme* (1839).

Scott, sitting on the right, entertains some literary cronies at his pseudo- manorial pile of Abbotsford. Painting by Thomas Faed.

THE PLOT THICKENS

Washington Irving *(1783–1859)— alongside* **James Fenimore Cooper***, the first internationally recognized American "man of letters"—gives the States cultural commodities like* Rip Van Winkle *and* The Legend of Sleepy Hollow*, in his affable, light-toned prose. The new nation's unofficial laureate is* **William Cullen Bryant** *(1794–1878)—positively Wordsworthian in his feelings for, and speculations on, nature.*

1782 The Montgolfier brothers discover that heat makes a silk bag buoyant and, in 1783, achieve the first ascent in a balloon of silk and paper.

1796 Edward Jenner, an English physician, performs the first successful vaccination against smallpox.

1825 Courtesan Harriette Wilson invites Wellington to pay not to be mentioned in her notorious—and fascinating—*Memoirs*. His reply: "Publish and be damned."

1760~1850

Gothic

From Udolpho to Wuthering Heights

What did an obscure Teutonic tribe do to deserve this? By bizarre etymological processes, the 7th-century invaders of Spain and Italy have mutated into the fey, flour-faced contemporary subculture whose dubious claim to distinction is the writing of Angela CARTER (1940–92). The main agent in this transformation was a literary genre that can be firstly accredited to the dilettante Horace WALPOLE (1717–97), writing back in 1764. The specters and clanking armor of The Castle of Otranto *came to him in a nightmare, he claimed. Its setting of ruined "Gothic" arches was an early harbinger of the historical consciousness that would preoccupy Scott et al.*

Walpole's fantasy encouraged other eccentrics to explore the dark side of Europe's "Enlightenment" imagination. William Beckford's singular life-story beats his Oriental romance *Vathek* (1786), while Ann Radcliffe's *The Mysteries of Udolpho* (1794) may well be best remembered as the target of Jane Austen's irony in *Northanger Abbey*. It was in the early 19th century, however, that a willingness to be taken wherever your nightmare might lead really came into its own as a literary principle.

Nightmare Abbey

The ultimate in Gothic titles? Actually, it's a parody of the whole vogue by Thomas Love Peacock (1785–1866), a good-humored satirist who still has a cult following in the present day.

Horace Vernet's painting (1839) of Gottfried Bürger's "Ballad of Lenore" (1774) defines the genre's lurid, ludicrous parameters.

1826 Joseph Nicéphore Niepce, pioneer of photography, produces the first permanent photograph.

1829 The Indian custom of suttee (the burning of widows) is banned.

1835 Advertisement: "Corsets 25/-. Patent caoutchouc instantaneous closing corsets ... the most extraordinary improvement that has ever been effected."

Mary Shelley at 19—the age at which she created *Frankenstein*.

In Germany, there were the frenetic, spook-ridden, fierily exciting short tales of *E. T. A. HOFFMANN* (1775–1822); the Polish Jan Potocki would adapt this kind of antirealism in his extraordinary *Manuscript Found at Saragossa*.

Concurrently, in Switzerland, *Mary SHELLEY* (1797–1851) hit on one of the great myths of modernity when she developed the fruits of a weekend writing contest (with her husband, Percy Bysshe, and Byron) into *Frankenstein* (1818). In Edinburgh, James Hogg's twisted take on Calvinist psychology in *The Confessions of a Justified Sinner* (1824) was equally dark and disturbing.

The "Gothick" genre became hugely popular, being distributed via circulating libraries such as that used by the *BRONTË* sisters. *Wuthering Heights* (1848), by *Emily* (1818–48), sets off within Gothic conventions—uncomprehending narrators reporting bizarre sadistic incidents in outlandish locations—but reaches out, with surefooted imaginative power, to become an enduring and universal myth of passion. *Jane Eyre* (1847) is equally dark and compulsive; but *Charlotte B.* (1816–55) is a more self-conscious writer—sophisticated by the stay in Brussels described in *Villette* (1853).

THE PLOT THICKENS

Gothic is writing trying to reclaim the primal power it had before myth became respectable "literature." It's bad and it's brilliant: witness its greatest monument, the atrocious mannerisms and astounding memorability of the poems and stories of **Edgar Allan Poe** *(1809–49). Poe, an itinerant New England journalist who would end his life in a tragic shambles of alcoholism, created some of the most enduring images of 19th-century writing (that is, for us now, some of the corniest): the cracking and breaking* The Fall of the House of Usher, The Raven *croaking* "Nevermore," *and* The Murders in the Rue Morgue, *a story which would introduce the murder mystery theme to fiction.*

An image from the thick of Gothic Romantic feeling, painted by Gustave Courbet (see p. 58).

1837 Sir Isaac Pitman's shorthand system comes into use; outside the U.S., this is still the most widely used shorthand.

1844 Christina Rossetti's *Goblin Market* is the Pre-Raphaelites' first successful publication.

1852-65 Samuel Fox introduces a curved steel frame and other design modifications to the umbrella.

1830~1870

Windy Monuments
The Forces of Nature

The Crash Course *principle of literary history is this: think what they were trying to do in their own time, before you worry what they look like now. It gets tricky in the case of Alfred, LORD TENNYSON (1809–92). That "comma LORD" for a start: that and the beard and locks. Here's a man, it seems, whose main* intention *was to become a literary monument. Even the extreme sonorous beauty of his verse seems designed to guarantee his enshrinement as Poet Laureate of Victorian England.*

Tennyson, given photographic apotheosis by his worshiper Julia Margaret Cameron.

What was he trying to communicate? Beneath the fine craftsmanship, an anxious low-spiritedness is the bottom line of the majestic "Tithonus" and *In Memoriam* (1833–50), the sequence mourning his friend Arthur Hallam—a gloom shot through, it's true, by wan glimmers of hope.

MEMO

Another break from Victorian stuffiness: Arthur Hugh Clough (1819–61), rattling off the broken-rhythmed, open-minded, conversational vivacity of *Amours de Voyage* and *Dipsychus*.

As they said to the anteater who won the lottery, "So why the long face?" *Matthew ARNOLD* (1822–88) had it too, surveying "Dover Beach" before he gave up poetry for criticism and lecturing.

Their blues were largely religious. God—fitfully shimmering through the clouds of Romanticism—seemed to have sunk below the horizon, leaving humanity to face a heavy drizzle of scientific skepticism. A similarly furrowed brow and carefully gathered mantle of literary dignity characterizes the French poet *Alfred DE VIGNY* (1797–1863).

1855 David Livingstone discovers the Victoria Falls and names them after Queen Victoria.

1859 Charles Darwin's *The Origin of Species*, propounding the theory of natural selection, provokes furious opposition.

1863 Louis Hannart invents an "improved clasp for gloves and other wearing apparel, for umbrellas, bags ..."; the press stud.

France, however, had *Victor Hugo* (1802–85)—a prodigious force of nature, from his youth an ebullient kicker-around of the poetic rulebook; a matchless lyricist of passion and political scorn; a dramatist whose stridently Romantic *Hernani* (1830) opened to pitched battles between foes and supporters in the stalls; a political exile on Jersey from the Second Empire, a proud prophetic presence (also, for contemporary tastes, a bit of a windbag). How much time these 19th-century types were prepared to lend to poetry! The years to write, the years to read. Hugo's "epic" treatment of humanity's cosmic destiny, *La Légende des siècles* (1859-77); "the greatest book of the 19th century," in its day. We humbly confess, O trusting *Crash Course* consumer, that we never quite reached the end. Stick to his lyrics.

No, nothing like this north of the English Channel. But there's *Robert Browning* (1812–89), an exuberantly unstuffy, reckless versifier compared with his rival Tennyson. Reckless, too, in his exploration of grotesque and extreme moral positions through his invention of the "dramatic monologue"— which also allows him to play out his historical fascinations with Italy. At least, there's Browning until he gets the big-book bug, and wastes his narrative talents on *The Ring and the Book* (1869)—twice the length of *Paradise Lost*, but utterly inert. Alternately, there's his wife *Elizabeth* née *Barrett* (1806–61)—an equally productive poet, and more highly regarded in her day.

Childe Roland

Is this Victorian England's greatest poem? Browning's "Childe Roland to the Dark Tower Came" has the medievalism that's quintessential to the era (vocab along the lines of "Faugh!," "scutcheons" etc.); always looks like it's about to be an allegory of religious faith without ever crassly becoming one; is lurid, grotesque, desperate, exciting; doesn't feel overstretched in length (Tennyson, please take note); is what it is, an extraordinary, charged verbal singularity, and unforgettable.

Millais' medieval fantasy *Sir Isumbras at the Ford* is thoroughly in the spirit of High Victorian poetry.

1830 French composer Hector Berlioz's first major work, the *Symphonie fantastique*, evokes a frustrated artist's opium-induced reveries.

1835 Danish writer Hans Christian Andersen publishes his *Tales Told for Children*, the first series of his fairytales.

1838 French artist Eugène Delacroix uses "divisionism," juxtaposing pure colors and allowing the viewer's eye to blend them.

1830~1860
Progress at Last!
Literary Dynamos

Comprehend, command, transform—these are the imperatives of mid-19th-century "progress," in science, imperialism, and industry: the age of the railroad and the steamship. In like fashion, there's a stupendous, clanking, accelerating vitality to the prose fiction of the era. Epitomized above all by the figure of Honoré DE BALZAC *(1799–1850)—the great man-mountain at work at his desk,*

Big man, big heart: Balzac, painted from a daguerreotype.

sweating away through the 1830s and 40s to nail down the whole social fabric of France in the panoramic series of novels collectively entitled La Comédie humaine *(take that, Dante!).*

MEMO

Meanwhile in German fiction, the scale is rather smaller: see the exquisite, post-Romantic stories of Adalbert Stifter (1805–68) or the *Bildungsroman* of Gottfried Keller, *Green Heinrich* (1855).

Gross and bumptious in his figure and energies; forever compoundly in debt and in love; profoundly generous in his creation of unforgettable characters. Balzac applies scientific—or pseudoscientific—methods to his material, which takes in political history, commercial practice, provincial smalltalk, and mystical speculation. The paradox is that, for all this effort toward contemporaneity, Balzac's intentions ran against the current of the age—which he

chastised for its reduction of all values to money values.

Paris was smothered with the steam of literary engines. Besides Balzac, there was "Alexandre Dumas & Co.," as jealous rivals dubbed the equally fast-firing author of *Les Trois Mousquetaires* (1844) and *Le Comte de Monte Cristo* (1845). This *DUMAS* (1802–70)—not to be confused with his son *Alexandre DUMAS* (1824–95), author of *La Dame aux camélias* (1848)—was working in the same line as Scott—historical romance—but, in his streamlined action narrative, distinctly improving on it (who said there's no such thing as progress

1846 Adolphe Sax, having combined the clarinet's single reed with the oboe's bore and fingering patterns, patents the saxophone in Paris.

1849 American inventor Walter Hunt is offered $400 for all rights to various shapes into which he twists an old piece of wire—including the safety pin.

1856 Louis Pasteur develops his germ theory of diseases.

in literature?). And, at the next platform, *Victor Hugo* (1802–85) had rolled into the fiction station, propelling his enormous creative powers into the medieval melodramas of *Notre-Dame-de-Paris* (1831)—enter Quasimodo—and, later on, the seething underworld of *Les Misérables* (1862).

Further along the concourse, *George Sand* (1804–76) and *Eugène Sue* (1804–75) were also offering the milling crowds romantic and melodramatic rides, with the sensationalism that other countries would learn to associate with the idea of "the French novel." Sand had plenty of personal material to draw on: *Elle et lui* (1859) is a thinly veiled account of her affair with Alfred de Musset, and *Un hiver à Majorque* describes an episode in her long-term relationship with the composer Frédéric Chopin.

THE PLOT THICKENS

The grand collected caboodle of Balzac's La Comédie humaine *splits into:* MORAL STUDIES. *"Scenes of Private Life," 27 stories, including* Le Père Goriot *(1835), introducing social-climbing protagonist Eugène de Rastignac, contrasted to sad old eponymous victim of moneymania;* "Scenes of Provincial Life," 12, *including* Eugénie Grandet *(1833), virtuous maiden caught between miserly dad and rotten suitor; "Scenes of Parisian Life," some 23, i.e.,* Le Cousin Pons *(1846), scrounging dilettante, expiring, falls prey to vulturish relations; scenes also, of "Political Life," "Military Life" (including* Les Chouans, *1829, first publication of the set), and "Country Life."* PHILOSOPHICAL STUDIES. 20 *stories, including* Le Chef d'oeuvre inconnu, *the definitive story about modern art, written back in 1831. O.K.? Get reading: see you in ten years' time!*

Scene from Nanteuil's illustrations for *Notre-Dame-de-Paris*.

1830 Louis-Philippe, last king of France, comes to power. His reign will be captured in the merciless caricatures of Honoré Daumier.

1851 Queen Victoria opens the Great Exhibition. The Crystal Palace is the world's largest glass-walled structure and will influence European railroad station design for decades.

1861 William Morris and associates set up the firm Morris, Marshall, Faulkner, and Co. to produce craftsman-made articles for the home.

1830~1870

Such a Thing As Society
"The Condition of England"

"Dizzy" before he became prime minister.

Before Thatcher, before Blair, England consisted of a stratosphere of classes. When an Englishman felt for himself, he played pool with his social status. Other people's accents, manners, appearances, and possessions were all clues in this endlessly obsessive concern. The English largely fiddled from anxiety, because their positions kept shifting in a jostling, mobile society.

That anxiety doesn't begin to explain the fantastic creative energy of *Charles Dickens* (1812–70), but it does help explain the context in which he became England's most popular novelist. A childhood experiencing respectability, then destitution (when his middle-class father was imprisoned for debt) supplies a rich fund of social observation that wins him early fame in *The Pickwick Papers* (1837). From *Oliver Twist* (1838) onward, his feeling for the heights and depths of society lands him a role as spokesman for the conscience of the nation—one he plays to the hilt. He takes aim at popular targets—fraudulent private schools, the law, bureaucracy—and speaks up for social compassion, often through tearjerking scenes; the audience loves him for it, not least at the readings that he frequently gives (and which proved the death of him).

Dickens tells the English about their own society. Benjamin Disraeli—later to run that society as prime minister—tells them how things were and ought to be in novels like *Sybil*, or the *Two Nations*

Dickens, in a quiet moment, thinks with compassion of the boy who has just done such a good job of shining his shoes.

1863 "Madame Rachel" opens a beauty salon in Bond Street, London. She is jailed after she attempts to blackmail her wealthy clients.

1868 J. P. Knight invents the first traffic signal, which is stationed outside the Houses of Parliament in London. It blows up, killing a policeman, and is not replaced.

1869 *The Subjection of Women*, a classic text advocating female emancipation, is the fruit of a long collaboration between John Stuart Mill and his wife-to-be, Harriet Taylor.

THE PLOT THICKENS

Sketches by Boz *(1836), journo pieces;* The Pickwick Papers *(1837), the comic genius arrives;* Oliver Twist *(1838), moralizing with grotesques;* Nicholas Nickleby *(1839), Dotheboys Hall, big mixed bag;* The Old Curiosity Shop *(1841), weep over Little Nell;* Barnaby Rudge *(1841), 18th-c. historical romance;* A Christmas Carol *(1843), Scrooge;* Martin Chuzzlewit *(1844), Pecksniff, Mrs. Gamp, slags off Yankees;* Dombey & Son *(1848), big "modern society" number;* David Copperfield *(1850), five-star Bildungsroman;* Bleak House *(1853), Jarndyce & Jarndyce, cosmic satirical genius;* Hard Times *(1854), up north, Gradgrind and his "facts";* Little Dorrit *(1858), debtors' prison, a tad somber;* A Tale of Two Cities *(1859), re French revo.;* Great Expectations *(1861), Pip, Mrs. Havisham, compact masterpiece;* Our Mutual Friend *(1865), love and money;* The Mystery of Edwin Drood *(1870)—unsolved when C. D. expires giving reading. Got all that?*

Thackeray's comic spirit also came through in his work as an illustrator. He worked for the magazine *Punch*, contributing articles and humorous sketches.

seen in his day as Dickens's rival. *William Makepeace* THACKERAY (1811–63), assembles a satiric vision of society at large in *Vanity Fair* (1848), woven around the figure of the unscrupulous climber Becky Sharp. But Thackeray is less a critic than an irreverent, inventive comic, working to the model of Fielding's novels (see p. 37).

Dickens, however, remains central to English culture because of the density of his imaginative prose—with its cluttered London streets, its wild relish in peculiarities and details, above all the way it coalesces into an enormous gallery of flamboyant characters. Dickens is an intense alternative world. There's no mistaking it for reality: it's far more real.

(1845). Elizabeth Gaskell brings working-class life and grievances to the fore in fiction for the first time in *Mary Barton* (1848), before moving on to the superbly realized village life of *Cranford* (1853) and the complex, masterly *Wives and Daughters* (1866). Meanwhile, the writer

1855 Gas ovens are marketed by the English firm of Smith and Phillips. They cost £25 each.

1864 W. G. Grace plays in his first county match at the age of 16, thus beginning a career in which he would become the greatest all-around cricketer ever.

1869 The Suez Canal opens, linking the Mediterranean with the Red Sea.

1855~1890

The Reality of Realism
Telling It How It Is

Dorothea marries Casaubon in *Middlemarch*.

"Reality"—let's make this clear—isn't real. It's a word we push at each other to promote what we think is important. What was important in the age of Pasteur, Maxwell, and Darwin was the scientist's grasp on physical matter; describing human life this way, stressing its grittier aspects, equaled "realism"—or so the critic Champfleury reckoned in 1857. (Dante and Rumi, see pp. 22–23, would have totally disagreed; so would most "Modernists," see below.)

As if words could wrap themselves, accurately and compactly, around every particle of existence: that's the spirit behind *Madame Bovary* (1857), the tour de force that led *Gustave FLAUBERT* (1821–80) to be hailed by critics as the great "realist" and to be prosecuted by the state for immorality. For some readers (i.e., this one) Flaubert's painstakingly assembled words choke the life out of things; but there's no denying their willful power, nor Flaubert's empathy for his

Scarlet woman
George Eliot flew in the face of Victorian proprieties in her own life, openly living with the prominent thinker George Henry Lewes, who was already married to another woman. For this she was ostracized by much of polite society, including her own pious brother.

Reality as seen in Robert Koehler's *The Strike* (1889).

1876 "Mr. Watson, come here, I want you." Alexander Graham Bell transmits the first message ever sent by telephone.

1889 Adolf Hitler is born in Austria.

1890 Sir James Frazer publishes *The Golden Bough: A Study in Comparative Religion*, proposing that all cultures pass from the magical, to the religious, to the scientific.

Zola's portrait of Cézanne, his oldest friend, in *L'Œuvre* (1881), led to their falling out.

provincial adulteress. The acquitted Flaubert paints more briskly and broadly in his sardonic tale-of-our-times, *L'Education sentimentale* (1869), and other specimens of his complex, disillusioned intelligence reach beyond "realism" altogether, for instance into Orientalist romance (*Salammbô*, 1862) and philosophic satire (*Bouvard et Pécuchet*, 1881).

Other writers, however, like Edmond and Jules Goncourt, pick up the "realist" (later, "naturalist") baton. Reality, by their account, mainly happens in the basement, where the lower classes slave and sweat. You need to observe them like laboratory specimens, even if you sympathize with their sufferings: this is the spirit in which *Émile* ZOLA (1840–1902) writes his début, *Thérèse Raquin*, in 1867, and the tremendously forceful series about the families Rougon and Macquart, which follows between 1871 and 1893. (For Flaubert's and Zola's friend Guy de Maupassant, see p. 68.)

Reality isn't real; but we still need the concept. God, thought *Marian* EVANS (1819–80), isn't there to judge us, but we

---

THE PLOT THICKENS

Reality, English style: the assumption that fiction ought to be about society (central to a broad swathe of English writing, down to British soap operas like The Archers*) is underlined by the productive* **Anthony Trollope** *(1815–82), who not only introduced the pillar mailbox to England, in his work for the Post Office, but introduced England to "Barsetshire" and to the political world of "the Pallisers" in two lengthy novel sequences (1855–67, 1864–80). Barsetshire is extremely like any other western county of Victoria's England in the middle of her reign, peopled by plausible individuals caught up in predictable predicaments—except that it is composed of thousands of pages of mellifluous, steady, comfortably enjoyable prose.*

---

must still be moral. She turns to the rural and small-town life of the Midlands of England, picking up on the type of "social" novel made popular by writers like Elizabeth Gaskell (see p. 57); and as "George Eliot," portrays the complexities of moral interaction in novels that culminate in the sober *Middlemarch* (1872). What is remarkable, given her background in abstruse German translations, is the plain, affecting poignancy of a tale like *The Mill on the Floss* (1860).

1850 Allan Pinkerton, American detective, founds the Pinkerton National Detective Agency to investigate cases of freight theft on the railroads.

1851 Isaac Singer (not to be confused with the writer, Isaac Bashevis Singer) designs the first practical sewing machine.

1853 Chef George Crum's boss complained that his chips were too thin, so in ironic response he shaved them paper thin and thus was the potato chip born!

1850~1890
How to Be American
Inventing a Nation

All nations are "invented" (or whatever modish academic term you prefer for getting people to subscribe to a common value), but the United States of America is more of a conscious construct than most. From the Puritan Founding Fathers, through Jefferson's Constitution, Americanness has always been a way of not falling into European habits. If the United States were to have a "national" literature, it would have to follow the same principle.

Uncle Tom

America's most popular —and controversial— novel of the 1850s: *Uncle Tom's Cabin* (1852) by Harriet Beecher Stowe. The book did so much for the antislavery cause, which would tear the States apart in the 1860s, that Abraham Lincoln greeted its author: "So you're the little woman who made the book that made the great war."

European habits, however, persist in the Americans we've mentioned before (see p. 49)—the Scottlike Fenimore Cooper, the Wordsworthian Bryant et al. It's only around 1850 that things start happening in American writing that would be inconceivable back in Europe.

It's that year that *Nathaniel HAWTHORNE* (1804–64) publishes *The Scarlet Letter*. Hawthorne's fictional territory is American psychological roots in Puritanism—this story of a stigmatized adulteress is set back in 17th-century New England. But that psychology—even if Hawthorne rejects it— affects his writing profoundly, opening up in it a feeling for allegory that had disappeared almost completely from the writing of mid-19th-century Old England.

A scene of heartrending (or nauseating) pathos from the controversial *Uncle Tom's Cabin*, as painted by Edwin Long.

1865 *Alice's Adventures in Wonderland* is written by English mathematician Lewis Carroll.

1878 Frontierwoman Martha Jane Canary (a.k.a. Calamity Jane) works tirelessly with smallpox victims in South Dakota, wearing men's clothing.

1890 Vincent van Gogh shoots himself in Auvers, France, and dies there two days later, age 37.

Herman MELVILLE (1819–91) looked up to Hawthorne's example: but his magnum opus is much weirder. A *whole lot* weirder. What can we call *Moby-Dick* (1851)? A novel? An encyclopedia of whaling lore? An epic tragedy? A Rabelaisian word-feast? A political allegory of the "ship of state?" A metaphysical allegory of humanity and God? All these things, and many more: the book's vast bulk can swallow all that critics throw at it, and in the 20th century they've thrown an awful lot. This critic would call it a nightmare of seasick rhetoric, but greater minds have called it the greatest. In its day, however,

THE PLOT THICKENS

An attempt at American literature, roots-style: The Song of Hiawatha *(1855) by* **Henry Longfellow** *(1807–82), prolific Harvard rhymester—Native American heritage product, served up in a memorably inane meter lifted from the Finnish* Kalevala *(see p. 47).*

the book bombed. Melville didn't recover his stride till just before his death, when he penned the visionary tome *Billy Budd* (1891).

But for definitive American originality, don't miss *Leaves of Grass* (1855). *Walt* WHITMAN (1819–92),

Whitman in 1890— by which time *Leaves of Grass* had seen six ever-expanding editions.

stretching out to hug the universe with tender phrases, writes like no other poet before him—except perhaps the Psalmists, Rumi, and Blake—but, where they sing of God, he sings of himself. Fond of himself, is Walt; but, democratically believing the next man's as good as he, he's fond of him too. The ideas may derive from the great American thinker *Ralph Waldo* EMERSON (1803–82), but the poetry is startling in its immediacy: "feel-good" writing, in the best sense.

1853-56 More
soldiers die of disease
than of their wounds
in the Crimean War.

1861 Leading
anarchist Mikhail
Bakunin escapes from
prison in Eastern Siberia.

1870 Dmitri Ivanovich
Mendeleev publishes *The
Principles of Chemistry*,
in which the 63 known
elements are arranged
into a periodic table.

1850~1900

Bearhugs

The Monumental Russians

*Let's head East. Here be giants.
Good old-fashioned Western European
literature has nothing of quite the
imaginative audacity of* War and
Peace, Anna Karenina, Crime and
Punishment, The Idiot, *or* The
Brothers Karamazov. *Thank God,
some may say. For some tastes, Ivan*
TURGENEV (1818–83) *is much more the
acceptable face of Russian fiction than
Leo* TOLSTOY (1828–1910) *and Fyodor*
DOSTOYEVSKY (1821–81). *There is the*

Leo Tolstoy in 1884—the
time of his soul-searchings, in
books like *What I Believe*.

exquisite artistic tact, and the Pushkinian intimacy of tone, in Fathers
and Sons *(1862) that earned Turgenev the respect of his friends Flaubert
and Henry James. The later Anton* CHEKHOV *(1860–1904), through the
ambivalent but archetypal predicaments presented in his plays and
short stories, and through a comparable human tenderness, has
become an even greater favorite with Western audiences.*

THE PLOT THICKENS

One foot in this world, one in the next:
Nikolai Gogol *(1809–52), comic
genius, publishes part 1 of the (despite
its title) hilariously lively masterpiece
Dead Souls (1842); writes part 2;
meets hellfire preacher, big change of
mind; part 2 goes up in flames, Gogol's
soul goes up to heaven ten days later.*

Leo Tolstoy and Fyodor Dostoyevsky,
however, can do what these guys can
do ("Can Dostoyevsky write *lightly?*"—
Yes. Read *The Eternal Husband*); but they
aren't satisfied with it. They are not
satisfied, in fact, until they have wrestled
with the world they describe and have
sent it reeling.

Tolstoy: landowner at Yasnaya Polyana,
army officer in Caucasus (scene,
incidentally, of Lermontov's wonderful
A Hero of Our Times, 1854) and Crimea.

1877-78 Peter Tchaikovsky, in turmoil after his disastrous marriage, finishes the opera *Eugene Onegin*, based on Aleksandr Pushkin's great novel in verse.

1881 Jews and their property are attacked by mobs in more than 200 pogroms, after the new Tsar Alexander III makes them the scapegoats for the murder of his father.

1897 Konstantin Stanislavsky co-founds the Moscow Art Theater, aiming to reach a wider public with more realistic productions of new work.

Writes up these experiences plus boyhood; moves on to whole Napoleonic invasion of Russia, complete with philosophy of history, in *W & P* (1863–69). Scribbles little number about adultery, *A. K.*, in another four years (1873–77). Hits midlife crisis: searches for God; gets sick of art. Can't help producing a bit more world-beating art (*Hadji Murad*, 1904, etc.). Expounds Christlike doctrines. Hailed as prophet. Runs away from wife, after 60 years' quarreling, to die at Astapovo ten days later: November 7, 1910.

Tolstoy—like Homer—seems to look at everything in life squarely in the face: freshly, wonderingly, passionately, comprehensively. But that involves *arguing* with life (and with death too).

Dostoyevsky: young St. Petersburg radical, 1840s. Writings high on Balzac and Dickens. Arrested as revolutionary, 1849: put before firing-squad; they were only joking. Sent to Siberia, doesn't get back till 1858. Writes up his time in *The House of the Dead* (1861).

He has now switched sides and decided he loves God and the Tsar. But this doesn't stop him from gambling his way into massive debts on trips to Western Europe (which, by the way, he censures severely). Writes his way out of them: *C & P* (1866), *The Twit* (1868), *The Possessed* (or *The*

Comic heroes

Russian fiction may be monumental, but it's also marvelously funny, with a unique tone of generous absurdity. Witness not only Gogol and Lermontov, but the immortal character of *Oblomov* (1859), created by Ivan Goncharov (1812-91). A young aristocrat, full of fine dreams, who unfortunately simply can't be bothered to get out of bed to enact any of them. This way he manages to lose the girl he's after, but tells himself: I'm a model of tranquility to the world … A hero for our own times?

Devils, 1872), *T B K* (1880). (NB. The twit—Prince Myshkin—is one of the rare fictional characters who manages to be at once virtuous and interesting.)

Dostoyevsky—like no one—looks straight through you, to the dark of your heart. Like the "terrible and wise spirit" in his great parable of "The Grand Inquisitor" (in *T B K*, book 5), he confronts you with the very core of your own nature by taking you to psychological extremes.

They Did Not Expect Him (1884): Repin dramatizes a political prisoner's return to his family from Siberia.

1852 Dr. Peter Mark Roget, English physician and scholar, publishes his *Thesaurus*, where words are grouped by subject matter.

1862 La Villette slaughterhouse opens in Paris in a building designed by Baron Haussman.

1871-73 German archaeologist Heinrich Schliemann rediscovers Troy.

1850s~1890

Symbols and Synesthesia
French Impressions

Verlaine shoots Rimbaud.

There are no rules. If there were, a provincial boy of 16 could not have revolutionized the terms of French poetry within three years, producing the most shatteringly original body of work in its history. Le Bateau ivre, Une Saison en enfer, *and* Les Illuminations *staked out a new reality of brutal, mystical, phantasmagorical ecstasy, pitched in a new diction and new meters. Having written them, Arthur RIMBAUD (1854–91) walked away from art, before he hit 20, to get on with life. He became a colonial entrepreneur in East Africa and died at age 37.*

Parnassians
Unlike Rimbaud or Verlaine, their contemporaries the "Parnassians"—poets led by Leconte de Lisle (1818–94)—rated restraint and classical dispassionateness. Their ancient cultures and fecund tropical scenes are summoned up in the fine-wrought, spirit-dampening pomp of Victorian monumental friezes.

There are no rules. But there are only a few situations in which such things can happen. The obvious factor in the Rimbaud phenomenon was that *Paul VERLAINE* (1844–96), a well-known poet and bohemian, took him up when he hit Paris from Charleville in 1871. (The two became lovers, set off for England—teaching English in Bournemouth!—then argued in Belgium. Verlaine shot and wounded Rimbaud; served time, during which he found God; then went back to the booze and whores.)

1879 Henry James publishes the novella *Daisy Miller*. In his lifetime, it will be more popular than anything else he ever writes.

1885 Untaught artist Henri ("le Douanier") Rousseau retires from his job as a customs inspector to devote his life to painting.

1888 John Dunlop, a Scottish veterinarian, fits his son's tricycle with inflated canvas-covered, sheet-rubber tubes—the first pneumatic tires.

But behind Verlaine, with his sneakily charming, impressionistic lyrics and his dither between sauciness and salvation, stands the centrally important *Charles BAUDELAIRE* (1821–67), whose criticism effectively created the French avant-garde; whose lyrics and "prose poems"– mostly in *Les Fleurs du mal* (1857)—brood compulsively on sin and synesthesia, desire, and decay, and, above all, on ennui, the spiritual sickness of an age of bourgeois mediocrity. Heir to Romanticism, and to Edgar Allan Poe; classicist in the precision of his verse; in his sexual emphases, realist (and, like Flaubert, prosecuted for this); forerunner of Symbolism.

> ### THE PLOT THICKENS
>
> *French poetry à la uruguayenne.* **Isidore Ducasse** *(1846–70), self-styled "comte de Lautréamont," hits Paris from Montevideo in 1867, and composes the satanic, protosurrealist prose–poetry potpourri of the* Chants de Maldoror *(published 1890).* **Jules Laforgue** *(1860–87) makes the same journey nine years later; writes dry but fantastical, self-mocking free verse (big influence on T. S. Eliot); likewise dies young.*

Paul and Art (on the left) hang out with some pals in 1872: painting by Fantin-Latour.

And this new "ism," enunciated in the wake of Rimbaud, means: don't state, suggest. To say just how it is gets it wrong: how it really is can only be hinted at. This is the doctrine of *Stéphane MALLARMÉ* (1842–98), author of *L'Après-Midi d'un faun* (1876; later made famous by Debussy's music). Mallarmé—as demure in lifestyle as Rimbaud had been wild—drew around himself a devoted following of Parisian writers in the 1880s, through the rigor with which he rethought poetry's relation to music and reality. His sonnets and lyrics are exact and circumspect, exquisitely tuned and shiftily inscrutable. This is the point in poetry's history at which "difficulty" sets in—or, to give it another name, "modernism." (See p. 89.)

1861 The American Civil War begins between the industrial North and the agrarian and feudal South.

1870 John Ruskin, art and literary critic, is elected the first Slade Professor of Art at Oxford University. An unwise attack on James McNeill Whistler in 1878 brings his public career to an end.

1881 Gilbert and Sullivan's satirical light opera *Patience* pokes fun at the cult of "Art for Art's sake" espoused by Oscar Wilde.

1860~1910s

Melancholy Muses
Housman, Hopkins, and Dickinson

Oscar. With that hairstyle, who else could it be?

BEAUTY. Now, there's a beautiful idea that is. Let's dream about beauty for a while. Mmmm … (Snore, snore.) Some such narcoleptic fantasy seems to have overmisted the mainstream of English poetry for more than a half-century in the wake of Tennyson's exquisite word-music and the sonorous inanity of Algernon Charles SWINBURNE (1837–1909). Beside Tennyson, there was the Paris-tinged influence of "Art for Art's Sake" doctrines from which Oscar WILDE (1854–1900) would extract the pith and satirize.

The figures who stand out from this mainstream of melodious melancholy are *Christina ROSSETTI* (1830–94), with her poignant lyrics of love and faith, and the tetchy classics don *A. E. HOUSMAN* (1859–1936), who in the pastoral quatrains of *A Shropshire Lad* (1896) manages to distill a weight of sophisticated pessimism into the plainspoken immediacy of a popular classic.

It remains a dismal era for English poetry, however—and things are little better across the pond, if we turn to the affable blandness of *James Russell LOWELL* (1819–91). Unless, that is, we look at it through the work of two poets who never saw publication in their lifetimes.

Beata Beatrix. Beauty as envisioned by Christina Rossetti's less talented brother Dante Gabriel R. (1828–82).

1896 *The Works of Max Beerbohm* is published, a book of essays and articles by the English caricaturist, critic, dandy, and wit.

1901 Jacques Brandenburger, a Swiss chemist, invents cellophane, a transparent, waterproof, protective covering for foodstuffs.

1909 Serge Pavlovich Diaghilev, Russian impresario, brings the Ballets Russes to Paris.

Beauty dreaming on beauty: Whistler's *Symphony in White* (1864).

Gerard Manley HOPKINS (1844–89) wrestled with his own poetic impulse—burning all the work he'd composed as an Oxford student when he became a Jesuit, a vocation that seems to have made his short life sharply unhappy. But his sonnets and lyrics—"The Windhover," "Pied Beauty," "Carrion Comfort"—are by far the most exhilarating of their age, because of the intensity with which he wrestled with God and God's creation, and with the customary methods of English scansion. Deriding its syllable-counting measuring of feet, his "sprung rhythm" is a kind of return to Old English poetic principles, but with a fresh, tight-packed intensity and complex charge of feeling.

Back to nature

The intense nature poetry of Hopkins and Hardy is matched in prose by the writings of Richard Jefferies (1848–87)—a passionate advocate of the rural values of his native Wiltshire; also, in *After London* (1885), author of one of the great visionary fantasies of modern civilization's downfall. W. H. Hudson (1841–1922) likewise combined an intense feeling for the English countryside (*A Shepherd's Life*, 1910) with futuristic utopianism (*The Crystal Age*, 1887) and a kind of protomagic realism in his tales of South America (*The Purple Land*, 1885).

THE PLOT THICKENS

Thomas Hardy *(1840–1928), after a profitable stint of novel writing (see p. 69), returned from 1896 to his first love, poetry. Harder to sell this stuff— so crabby, stiff, eccentric in its diction and meters it seemed to most poetic contemporaries. Yet his large body of short lyrics, wistful but wonderfully observant, has grown in stature over the 20th century as the others have declined. They seem more sincere; more necessary. The same can't yet be said for T.H.'s magnum opus, an enormous and enormously unread verse drama about the Napoleonic Wars entitled* The Dynasts *(1904–8). Maybe it'll come into its own in the 21st century?*

In Massachusetts, *Emily* DICKINSON (1830–86) presents a yet more daunting figure of internalized struggle. Defiantly reclusive, she plunges into the experience of meditation in a manner unprecedented by any previous poet, producing spare, muttered verses of sardonic spiritual asperity that seem to probe into the quality of the silences and the blank paper surrounding them: a terrifying, inside-out poetic world.

She early abandons all efforts to publish, leaving great masses of material to be discovered by her sister after her death; critics are still coming to terms with its originality.

1872 A cuneiform tablet from 3000 B.C. is found to give a description of a great flood that closely corresponds to the biblical one.

1875 Madame Blavatsky, initiated into Oriental occultism in Asia, cofounds the Theosophical Society; adherents include W. B. Yeats, Annie Besant, and Rudolf Steiner.

1881 Henrik Ibsen's naturalistic play about the evils of society, *Ghosts*, provokes a storm of outrage in Britain after a single performance.

1886 "The pause that refreshes," a new cocaine-based remedy for headaches, is marketed as Coca Cola.

1870s~1900

The Nature of Naturalism
Prostitution, Poverty, and Really Bad Luck

Nothing could be more naturalistic than a terminal illness. Painting by Henry Geoffroy.

Realism (see pp. 58–9) was the biggest noise in later 19th-century fiction. To represent the substance of life accurately through a novel: this was a compelling challenge, summoning up hundreds of shelves full of imaginative effort—much of it from novelists who'd made their reputations before the ethos became prevalent. Spain's equivalent to Balzac and Dickens, the prodigious Benito Pérez Galdós, moved on from historical novels to give a vast and exquisitely detailed picture of Madrid life in Fortunata and Jacinta *(1886–87). In Berlin, Theodor Fontane, starting late on novel writing at 59, achieved a tragedy of adultery comparable to* Madame Bovary *and* Anna Karenina *through the deployment of observed detail and conversational nuance in his final* Effi Briest *(1895).*

Realism implied more than simple correspondence to the observed facts, however. As it led into "naturalism" in the hands of Zola in the 1870s, it became a vision; a pseudo-scientific vision of human nature—inspecting the human animal to find it ruled by lust, greed, and criminality. *Thérèse Raquin* (1867) is generally acknowledged as the first

War coverage
Stephen Crane went on from *Maggie: A Girl of the Streets*, with its brutally grim picture of New York tenement squalor, to write *The Red Badge of Courage* (1895)—a soldier's-eye view that is often seen as the definitive novel about the American Civil War. All the smarter since Crane had never seen battle.

"naturalistic" novel, and there followed the descriptions of life in a mining community in *Germinal* (1885) and country peasants in *La Terre* (1887). Zola's friend and Flaubert's protégé, Guy de MAUPASSANT (1850–93), gave the sharpest, clearest-eyed expression of this disillusionment in his remorselessly powerful short stories. Hard fates await his

1890s Henri de Toulouse-Lautrec celebrates dancers Jane Avril and Loie Fuller and singers Aristide Bruant and Yvette Guilbert in his striking and innovative posters.

1899 British imperialism clashes with Afrikaner nationalism in the Boer War; guerrilla warfare, concentration camps, and a legacy of bitterness.

protagonists, like the provincial prostitute of *Boule-de-suif* (1880), the story that made his name. A harder fate awaited their creator, who would go to an early death, insane with syphilis.

French naturalism led the way for other plunges into the grim and grimy—like *Maggie: A Girl of the Streets* (1893) by the brilliant, short-lived *Stephen CRANE* (1871–1900) (see box), or *New Grub Street* (1891), George Gissing's agonizing account of the poverty induced by literary hackwork. (Publishers, please read.) Its post-Darwinian, atheistic premises also led to the truly cosmic pessimism shared by two of the greatest novelists of the gloom-ridden fin-de-siècle.

Meanwhile, in Italy, *Giovanni VERGA* (1840–1922) wrapped an awesomely harsh, exact prose around the humble lives of small-time Sicilian peasants, exposing their modest aspirations to the meanness of their fellow men and the meaningless mockery of fate: *I Malavoglia* (1881) and *Mastro-don Gesualdo* (1889) remain bitter, invigorating masterpieces; Fernet-Branca reading.

In England, *Thomas HARDY* (1840–1928) was equally glum about the general outlook—larding his narratives with crashingly insistent instances of bad luck for all and sundry. But what stays with the reader from novels like *Far from the Madding Crowd* (1874) or *Tess of the D'Urbervilles* (1891) is instead Hardy's

THE PLOT THICKENS

Thomas Hardy *started as an architect and aimed to be a poet; his vastly productive excursion into novel and short-story writing from 1871 ended with* Jude the Obscure *(1895), a strident assault on the social and religious conventions of Victorian England that met with an outcry, being publicly burned by bishops. Either with his fingers burned, or his fictional interests burned out, H. reverted to poetry; see page 67.*

encompassing tenderness toward his own creations—the personally branded West Country he names "Wessex," and in particular his lovingly imagined heroines. (A tenderness that, his biographers suggest, he failed to extend to the women who actually shared his life.)

Nastassia Kinski is *Tess* (1979). Director Polanski does his best to be Naturalist painter Millet.

1860 *Godey's Ladies' Book* advises American women that tomatoes should be cooked for at least three hours.

1871 33,000 die in the siege of the Paris Commune.

1883 The Special Branch of the Metropolitan Police is set up in London to protect state personages and suppress terrorism.

1860~1900
Escape! Adventure! Mystery!
Jobs for the Boys

Wilkie Collins.

Realism may have been the biggest noise in later 19th-century fiction, but there were no end of descants and discords vying for the reader's attention. The frenetic imagination of Dickens constantly transcends "everyday reality"; so does that of his friend Wilkie COLLINS *(1824–89). Collins, furiously scribbling his way through doses of opium, brings a Gothic feel for the uncanny and for convoluted secrecy to* The Woman in White *(1860) and* The Moonstone *(1868)—and in doing so, creates the hugely popular "sensation novel," a prototype for the genres of the murder mystery and the thriller.*

I n the same period, *Jules* VERNE (1828–1905), clumsy fisted in his prose but soaring in his vision of technological possibilities, opens up the idea of "science fiction" with *Voyage au centre de la terre* (1864). On either side of "mundane reality" lay the green pastures seemingly offered to the writer by two grand Victorian projects—colonialism and childhood. From a colonial experience of New Zealand, *Samuel* BUTLER (1835–1902) returns to upend all the conventions of contemporary society in his fantasy island of *Erewhon* (1872). Still more intellectually subversive is the comprehensive dream-satire of Victorian

---

THE PLOT THICKENS

Dracula (1897) was the Gothic creation of **Bram Stoker** *(1847–1912), Irish theatrical touring manager; the book is still a compulsively strange read, with its amassed research and lurid sexuality, but Stoker produced no follow-ups of note. Sherlock Holmes seems almost the creator rather than the creation of* **Arthur Conan Doyle** *(1859–1930)—whose stories appeared in* Strand *magazine from 1887 onward. After* The Hound of the Baskervilles *(1902) A.C.D. eventually escaped Sherlock and Watson to pen the lumbering paleontological fantasy of* The Lost World *(1912) and to embarrass his admirers by giving credence to "photographs of fairies" faked by two little girls.*

1888 An anonymous serial killer, Jack the Ripper, murders and eviscerates the first of (at least) five prostitutes he is to kill over the next three years.

1891 English roulette player Charles de Ville Wells "breaks the bank" at Monte Carlo six times in three days. He will die, penniless, in 1926.

1893 Whitcomb L. Judson invents the Hookless Fastener (or zip), comprising two thin metal chains that can be locked together with a metal slider.

Holmes' twilit London, evoked by Atkinson Grimshaw.

culture that *Lewis CARROLL* (a.k.a. Charles Dodgson; 1832–98) introduces into his testimonies of diverted passion for a prepubescent girl, *Alice in Wonderland* (1865) and *Through the Looking-Glass* (1871). In the soggier imaginative climate of the 1880s, *Rider HAGGARD* (1856–1925) uses his imperialist's knowledge of Africa (romanticizing the land, patronizing the inhabitants)

when he attempts to write "the best boys' story ever," *King Solomon's Mines* (1886). Haggard was competing with *Treasure Island* (1883). *Robert Louis STEVENSON* (1850–94) maps out a new territory of "adventure," for adult readers as much as children. Edinburgh-bred, this prolific and self-declared antirealist died at age 44 in Samoa, having given a new vigor to historical romance and to the Gothic manner—above all in *The Strange Case of Dr. Jekyll and Mr. Hyde* (1886). The split personality motif would join with the symbolist aestheticism of the 1880s—explored and found wanting in *A rebours* (*Against the Grain*; 1884) by Joris-Karl Huysmans—in Oscar Wilde's only novel, *The Picture of Dorian Gray* (1890).

Many of these escapes from the here-and-now have sunk so deep and broad into the popular imagination as not to need the status of "literature." None more so than two figures who stalk the world in a thousand reanimations, detached from their creators—Dracula and Sherlock Holmes.

Moonfleet

In Robert Louis Stevenson's footsteps, but written in commanding prose of dense, driving intelligence: John Meade Falkner's superb historical adventure *Moonfleet* (1898). Meade Falkner, a scholar who strangely went on to head a leading British armaments firm, also wrote the fascinating, Hardyesque *The Nebuly Coat* (1903).

A freestanding, one-legged fictional creation: Stevenson's Long John Silver.

1860s~1900

Frontiersmen
Colonial Writing

Every land that looks remote and unreal to us here— wherever we happen to be—feels like immediate fact to someone else. This obvious truth starts to impinge on the readers of Europe as writers follow traders and soldiers to the colonies. Marcus Clarke, for instance, produces the first great authentic account on the realities of life in penal Australia in For the Term of his Natural Life *(1874). Douwes Dekker, styling himself "Multatuli," gives a convoluted indictment of Dutch rule in Java in his autobiographical* Max Havelaar *(1860). Olive Schreiner not only introduces the British public to life in the Cape in* The Story of an African Farm *(1883) but also sounds a bold new note of feminism to her fictionalization.*

Colonial poetry
Henry Kendall and Linsay Gordon are among the first to give Australia a distinctive national voice, along with Andrew "Banjo" Patterson; Archibald Lampman is your man if you're (Anglophone) Canadian.

"Banjo" Patterson writing his Bush Ballads.

Kipling, "poet of the Empire," rattles off a press report from the front line of the Boer War in 1900.

This is in contrast to the patriarchal values that run through the novels— and namestyle—of her contemporary *"Mrs. Humphry WARD"* (1851–1920).

Much of this stuff is valuable precisely because it's less imaginative creation than reportage. Two writers, however, make the experience of the frontier into totally original art. *Rudyard KIPLING* (1865–1936), born in Bombay, lived in London from 1889 and settled the Indian continent permanently on the British imagination—the land of the working-class privates who speak out in the

1880 The first electric street lighting is introduced in New York.

1895 King Camp Gillette invents the safety razor; 90,000 will have been sold by 1904.

1899 Scott Joplin composes the most famous piano rag, his *Maple Leaf Rag*.

Barrack-room Ballads (1892), of the bazaars and fakirs of *Kim* (1901), and, most famously, of *The Jungle Book* (1894) and the *Just So Stories* (1902). Reaching for his subjects intimately and intuitively, Kipling at best extends the range of English writing in masterly fashion; at worst, is whimsical and imperialistically sententious.

Twain: his many great lines grace every modern Dictionary of Quotations.

Meanwhile, a whole swathe of American experience—far away from the New England so comfortably described in the novels of *William Dean HOWELLS* (1837–1920)—lay inarticulate until *Samuel Langhorne CLEMENS* (1835–1910) found his voice. Styling himself Mark Twain after a cry of the Mississippi boatmen (meaning "We've reached two fathoms"), he made the river his backyard

THE PLOT THICKENS

*Another wit of the West: the Californian **Ambrose Bierce** (1842–?1914), Twain's rival in cynicism, a veteran of the Civil War who shot to kill in all directions in the grandiloquently debunking* Devil's Dictionary—*sample definitions include "bore": a person who talks when you wish him to listen—was for years more famous for having disappeared without a trace, on a mysterious visit to Mexico, at the age of 72.*

in the great *Huckleberry Finn*. With its swift, sure action and diction, with its keen feel for river sensations and river people, the novel introduces a new "frontier" freshness to writing in English—even though that freshness shades into pathos and moral ambivalence. The novel, like *Pudd'nhead Wilson* (1889), is poised between the comedy that was Twain's mainstay and the pessimism that would lower over his later work. (Twain is immortal as the man who was able to cable the Associated Press office "The report of my death was an exaggeration.")

1885-88 Sir Richard Burton publishes his translation of the *Arabian Nights*.

1886 In a rash moment, Henry James writes to the editor of the *Pall Mall Gazette* that "the reading of the newspaper is a pernicious habit, and the father of all idleness and laxity."

1889 "Obvious quackery" says eminent British Egyptologist Frank Griffith on deciphering contraceptive advice in an ancient papyrus.

1880s~1905

Soul-Searching
The Rise of Psychology

Joseph Conrad.

Early in his career, Dostoyevsky—respinning the gloriously mad 1836 story by Gogol in which The Nose escapes its owner to lead a separate life—wrote a book called The Double *(1846). This tale of a doppelgänger—a bit like Hogg's* Justified Sinner *(see p. 51)—is his first, roundabout treatment of the idea that you do not understand yourself. Whatever you tell yourself about your intentions, they are really formed by deep-repressed passions that it would terrify you to acknowledge: so you project these feelings onto other persons.*

Conrad

He speaks like no one else, from his 20 years at sea, for the life of ships and ports and storms; but more than this, he broods on the precarious honor of men who find themselves isolated in alien lands. In doing so, he uncovers, like Dostoyevsky, the crux of terror where psychology intersects with politics: see *Lord Jim* (1900), *Nostromo* (1904), *The Secret Agent* (1907), and above all the great parable of colonialism, *Heart of Darkness* (1902).

This idea starts to bite into Western European writing from the 1880s. Not only in other doppelgänger stories—*Jekyll and Hyde*, *Dorian Gray*—but also in "realist" fiction like *La Regenta* (1888), the great tale of sexual tension and religious neurosis in a provincial Spanish town, by Leopoldo ALAS (1852–1901).

This was the age when Scandinavia—hitherto chiefly famous for the tales of Hans Christian Andersen—

"The Master," as rendered by fellow American expat John Singer Sargent.

began to export angst, as served up by the dramatists Henrik Ibsen and August Strindberg. Ibsen, stripping away the seemliness of Norwegian bourgeois life to expose the truths it denied, and Strindberg the Swede, with his visions of hysterical sexuality, set a context ripe for Freud's teachings of the early 20th century. People were turning in on themselves in a new way: taking the microscope to the soul.

1901 Herbert Booth patents the vacuum cleaner. The first large horse-drawn contraption has an 800-foot hose; carpets become 50% lighter and horses bolt at the noise.

1904 American-born Isadora Duncan dances in the ruins of the Theater of Dionysus in Athens.

1908 Moviemakers Léon Gaumont and Charles Pathé produce the first newsreel.

The well-heeled caught off guard: a Jamesian moment in Sargent's *Boat Party*.

social realities, true to his reverence for George Eliot, Flaubert, and Turgenev; on another, spinning yarns (i.e., *The Turn of the Screw*, 1898) like his friend Robert Louis Stevenson; on another yet, following his brother William James—a founder of modern psychology—to probe deep into motivation and the texture of conscious experience. It's the last of these, as displayed in *The Wings of the Dove* (1902), that makes him stand out as one of the harbingers of 20th-century "modernist" fiction.

All this bears on the complex career of one of America's most complex intelligences, *Henry JAMES* (1843–1916). It's customary to chop "the Master" into three, following the Stuart dynasty. "James the First" writes up mandarin Boston society and its ambivalent relations with the old continent—as in *The Portrait of a Lady* (1881). "James the Second," frequenting the top literary circles of London and Paris, moves in on English subject matter—as in *The Tragic Muse* (1890). Finally, "James the Old Pretender" is the mannered and imperiously contorted stylist of *The Golden Bowl* (1904), "a hippopotamus straining to pick a daisy," as H. G. Wells memorably described him.

But James splits other ways also—on one side scrupulously representing moral and

---

THE PLOT THICKENS

The Russian domination of 19th-century Poland produced three diverse literary reactions. **Henryk Sienkiewicz** *(1846–1916) reacted with historical romances such as* Quo Vadis? *(1896)—knocking the Roman Empire to hit at the Russian—while* **Boleslaw Prus** *(1845–1912) wrote contemporary naturalism with a vengeance—making the central image of* The Doll *(1890), with its complexities of commerce and politics, the marionettes in a Warsaw department store window. And* **Jozef Korzeniowski** *(1854–1924) sailed away from his native land for good— to end up, by one of the strangest literary destinies, as the major English novelist* **Joseph Conrad**.

1900 Oscar Wilde, Irish dramatist, verse writer, and storyteller, dies, age 44, in a small hotel in Paris. Only seven people attend his funeral.

1902 French moviemaker Georges Méliès produces *A Trip to the Moon.*

1904 In Dublin, Miss Annie E. F. Horniman takes out a 99-year lease on a music hall and adjacent morgue and the Abbey Theatre is born.

1900~1915

Cushy

Edwardian Novelists

Houses built in Britain's Edwardian era (1901–10) have a sleek self-satisfaction: solid, comfortable, yet decked with a faintly ironic, knowing mock-tudoring. So it is with the period's realist fiction. At its best, as in the novels of Arnold BENNETT *(1867–1931), it's built on a deep foundation of amused interest in the lives of ordinary people. Concentrating on the industrial "potteries" towns in* The Old Wives' Tale *(1908) and* Clayhanger *(1910), Bennett is masterfully sure of his ground, but unassertive in his technique.*

March of the moustaches (1): W. Somerset Maugham.

L ikewise, W. Somerset MAUGHAM (1874–1965) turns life (and unhappy love) into prose with agonizing

efficiency in his autobiographical masterpiece, *Of Human Bondage* (1915). (Somerset Maugham went on through a long career to entertain with sharply turned short stories, largely in colonial settings; but, for our purposes, obligingly and disarmingly summed himself up as "in the very first row of the second-raters.")

But a kind of trite, smirking canniness comes to the fore in John Galsworthy's highly readable account of the English

1910 D. H. Lawrence's mother sees an advance copy of his first novel, *The White Peacock*, shortly before her death.

1911 To encourage passengers to use the new escalators at London's Earls Court station, a man with a wooden leg is paid to ride them and demonstrate their safety.

1913 Caresse Crosby, American socialite, assembles two handkerchiefs and some ribbon and comes up with the "Backless Brassière"; she will sell the patent for $15,000.

upper middle classes, *The Forsyte Saga*, which appeared from 1906. This prewar world of *rentier* indolence and indulgent passions would get its finest portrayal in *The Good Soldier* (1915)—a Chinese-box narrative of breathtaking ingenuity and tragic power, into which *Ford MADOX FORD* (1873–1939) poured all the sophistication that came from his position at the epicenter of London literary life.

Yet Edwardian writing is also tinged with vague, unfocused optimisms and uncertainties about the new century. Thus *H. G. WELLS* (1866–1946) veers between the suburban naturalism of *The History of Mr. Polly* (1910) and the visionary anxieties of his science-fictional short stories—paralleling the reach of his fellow in "Fabian" socialism, *George Bernard SHAW* (1856–1950), who drily dramatizes not only contemporary dilemmas (*Major Barbara*, 1906),

George Joy's *Bayswater Omnibus* pictures English society at the end of Victoria's reign.

> ### THE PLOT THICKENS
>
> *Somewhere beyond cushioned, clubbable literary London lay— what?—real life? That's the possibility that wistfully attracted* **E. M. Forster** *(1879–1970). Often witty, too often blathering, Forster was a homosexual whose repression fired his finest earlier novel,* The Longest Journey *(1907); forget the embarrassingly portentous* Howards End *(1910).*

March of the moustaches (2): H. G. Wells.

but also historical episodes (*Caesar and Cleopatra*, 1901) and far-flung futures (*Back to Methuselah*, 1921). Another critic and wit of an era full of them, *G. K. CHESTERTON* (1874–1936), reaches with one hand for the comforts of "Merry England" (accompanied by his anti-Semitic chum Hilaire Belloc, "two buttocks of one bum"), while stretching out the other to the possibilities of anarchism in *The Man Who Was Thursday* (1908).

1905 The first public performance of Bernard Shaw's *Mrs. Warren's Profession* ends with the arrest of all concerned.

1906 San Francisco is shaken by an earthquake, followed by five days of fire.

1909 Filippo Tomasso Marinetti launches futurism; art must break with the past, embrace modern technology, and abandon earlier structures.

1900~1920s

Artistic Agonies
Rilke, Mann, Joyce, and Yeats

Rilke (right) soul-bonding with a Russian poet, 1900.

"I AM NOT LIKE YOU. I am a writer, an artist. My path is difficult and lonely, and you are unlikely to understand me, but what I produce redeems this life that slips through your hands ... or rather, perhaps it fails to do so ... but I reserve the right to fail. I am an artist."
That's the style in which modernism (following Baudelaire, but ultimately following the Romantics) offered scribblers a sense of mission. Don't mock: it could produce the goods. Read Rainer Maria RILKE (1875–1926). Read him, if you can, in his native German, because he transforms that linguistic heap of bricks into a clear-flowing stream of liquid intelligence.

If you can't, the *New Poems* (1907, 1908) and the awesome, daunting *Duino Elegies* (1922) still offer uniquely mobile, probing meditations about objects, spaces, people, animals, existence, and art. Rilke is the artist's artist par excellence; though he achieved this eminence by a somewhat unusual itinerant lifestyle, sponging off duchesses. (Read

MEMO

Essential Rilke: the *New Poems*, above all "Archaic Torso of Apollo," "The Bowl of Roses," "Orpheus, Eurydice, Hermes." (His best translations yet come from Stephen Cohn.) Essential Yeats: "Easter 1916," "Byzantium," "Among School Children."

him, finally, because he's this writer's favorite poet.)

I am an artist, firstly if not lastly, because I know how to represent things. Thus *Thomas MANN* (1875–1955) sets out his credentials in his first novel *Buddenbrooks* (1900)—a superbly observed saga of an industrial family's decline. He goes on to ruminate magisterially, expansively (you could say verbosely), on art and

1911 Norwegian explorer Roald Amundsen and Briton Robert Scott vie to reach the South Pole first. Amundsen wins the race; Scott and his party lose their lives.

1917 Leonard and Virginia Woolf buy a small hand press for £19.5s.5d., and install it in their dining-room. The Hogarth Press begins its illustrious career.

1920s American Michael Cullen plans "monstrous stores … away from the high-rent districts" and opens the first supermarket in Jamaica, New York.

the changing social order in weighty parables like *The Magic Mountain* (1924) and *Doctor Faustus* (1947)—on the way throwing off his most poignant vision of an artist's predicament in the brief *Death in Venice* (1911).

Sheer representational prowess is likewise the pitch on which *James JOYCE* (1882–1941) starts his extraordinary career, in the short stories of *Dubliners* (1914) and the unfolding self-definition of *Portrait of the Artist as a Young Man* (1915)—ending with his resolve to forge in his soul "the uncreated conscience of my race" (read on, p. 90).

That reciprocal tension between the artist's destiny and the nation's also comes to the fore in the other figure who made Ireland central to modern world literature. The poetry of *William Butler YEATS* (1865–1939), gradually emerging from

THE PLOT THICKENS

Voice of his people: **Rabindranath Tagore** *(1865–1941), much admired by Yeats, performed a comparable role in Bengal, representing not only in Bengali but in English the experience and imaginative values of his people; in the poems of* Gitanjali *(1912), and in the prose of* The Home and the World *(1919). In the Punjab,* **Muhammad Iqbal** *(1875–1938) is a slightly similar figure, an Islamic modernist writing in Persian and Urdu; though his content is more philosophical.*

the mists of a fey, symbolistic "Celtic Revival" and from his hapless passion for the beautiful zealot Maud Gonne, takes on a commanding urgency in the convulsions that led to Irish independence in 1921: his voice, always finely melodious, becomes at once keener and subtler, more comprehensive, and more innovative. It's perhaps faintly to be regretted that writing the most unforgettable lyrics in 20th-century English poetry entails bogus mysticism, sentential reaction, and pompous self-glorification by the wheelbarrowload; but who said poets should be nice?

Thomas Mann in 1947, sipping a Cinzano in Californian exile. His opposition to the Nazis made it prudent to leave Germany in the 1930s.

1911 Ernest Rutherford arrives at the nuclear theory of the atom.

1914 E. M. Forster's novel *Maurice*, a frank depiction of homosexuality, is circulated privately and will not be published until 1971.

1918 Pop-up toasters are invented by Charles St ite.

1910~1925
Mister Literature
Pocketbook Proust

Admit it: you picked up this little book because you wanted a quick crib to the work of Marcel PROUST (1871–1922). Because Proust, as we all know, is Mr. Literature himself. Because literature, as we all know, is deadly important, but life's just too short to read the stuff.

Monsieur Proust, the elegant aesthete who also wrote a bit.

THE PLOT THICKENS

*Exemplary eminence of French modernism: Mallarmé's most distinguished disciple, **Paul Valéry** (1871–1945). Ultrasmart young contender (Monsieur Teste, 1896); then shuts up for 15 years, loftily cogitating on a sinecure employment. Comeback in 1917, vouchsafing verse of impeccable sonorous inscrutability to widespread plaudits. Journals underline intellectual mandarin status. Top contribution to French literary stock: Le Cimetière marin (1920), beautiful, even moving.*

to pick up a pen. Go back to *À la recherche du temps perdu* (published 1913–27): sure, you will fall asleep somewhere in the world-encompassing three-page sentences, but persevere. You will discover the finest-textured, most brightly colored, above all *funniest* account ever given of love, jealousy, and everything else that makes life worth living.

Proust, writing from his own experience, enhances the quality of his readers' experiences because he is aware of his own absurdities and limitations. He played the role of a pampered, snobbish aesthete in the youth preceding the self-imposed Parisian seclusion in which he wrote his masterpiece. (Night by night, in a cork-lined room tailored to his hypochondrias, occasionally emerging for sadomasochistic diversion.) Reviewing that past life to

Fair enough. But look: Proust is better than literature—the way we usually know it, with all the little stupidities and conventions we allow fiction to give it breathing space. He is simply the most dazzling, comprehensive intelligence ever

1921 "Coco" Chanel, French couturière, introduces a new perfume, Chanel No. 5.

1922 Edith Sitwell recites *Façade*, a sequence of poems, with musical accompaniment by British composer William Walton.

1925 Lucky Strike cigarettes are launched with the slogan "Reach for a Lucky instead of a sweet."

comprehend and redeem it, he lends his bisexuality to the charming but louche "Baron de Charlus," his edgy Jewishness to the insufferably pushy "Bloch," his artistic strivings to the writer "Bergotte," his romantic wistfulness to the dapper socialite "Swann," while focusing his social aspirations on the elegance of the "Duchesse de Guermantes"—among a profusion of composite portraits of his acquaintance.

Yet all the time, his hopes are philosophical: he wants, somehow, to seize the essence of the reality he lives within. To find how he makes such an idea meaningful, you need to pass through a succession of infatuations (chiefly, for the unapproachable "Gilberte" and the unreliable, possibly lesbian "Albertine") and digressions (about everything from madeleines to telephones) to the concluding volume, "Le Temps retrouvé." There is a kind of circularity: he discovers that to make that life meaningful, he must write this book. But having done so, Proust has made the world a larger and more interesting place.

Love on a small scale
The hauntingly evoked adolescent romance of *Le Grand Meaulnes* (1913) is poised between yearning fantasy and sober reality. The one-of-a-kind masterpiece of Alain-Fournier (1886–1914), killed in the first months of the Great War.

The other great innovator in early 20th-century French fiction, besides Proust, is *André GIDE* (1869–1951). Like Proust, fascinated by his own multifariousness (read his *Journals*); like Proust, bisexual in his interests. But unlike him, spreading his energetic intelligence restlessly into a host of different forms: subversive teasers like *Les Caves du Vatican* (1914), "récits" (narratives focused on one character) like *La Porte étroite* (1911), and the clever-clever, self-referential metafiction of *Les Faux-monnayeurs* (1926). Initially scandalizing bien-pensant opinion, he ended up a major public voice, awarded the Nobel Prize in 1947.

André Gide, his head resting on his hand, with friends at Saint Cloud, as painted by Theo van Rysselberghe.

1911 The *Mona Lisa* is stolen from the Louvre in Paris.

1913 Stravinsky's *Le Sacre du Printemps (The Rite of Spring)* causes a scandal at its first performance.

1917 Charlie Chaplin signs the first-ever million-dollar film contract.

1910~1935

Life, Consciousness, etc.
Lawrence and the Big Bad Woolf

Wasn't some genteel Edwardian soul—I think it was E. M. Forster—muttering something back on page 77 about his hankerings after "real life?" Well, here's real life. It comes from Eastwood, Nottinghamshire. It sweats, throbs, fucks. It loves people, it gets mad at them.

Lawrence's *Rainbow* was controversially torrid for its time (1915).

It sees through to the heart with surpassing tenderness, or drivels like a delirious drunk. It also, in *Sons and Lovers* (1913), writes one of the most searingly powerful novels of passion and class sensibility in British literature.

After this early success and apart from his many wonderful poems and short stories (e.g., *The Man Who Died*), D. H. LAWRENCE (1885–1930) is—for this reader at least—a good-bad experience, half the most stimulating "voice" in British writing since Dickens, half a phony prophet of blood and semen. His furious trajectory through the range of British society and across the width of the globe is a splutter of brilliance and dross. But it's the need for

such a "priest of love" that counts historically. There had been precursors for the sort of role Lawrence played. Americans like Whitman and Twain, whom he intently studied; and various writers embodying the brute vitality, "beyond good and evil," of Nietzsche's massively influential philosophy. *Knut HAMSUN* (1859–1952), for instance, the unpleasant but compelling author of *Hunger* (1890); *Gabriele D'ANNUNZIO* (1863–1938), the bombastic Italian egotist; *Jack LONDON* (1876–1916),

Jack London in the heyday of his success.

1920 Margaret Anderson, editor of *The Little Review*, serializes James Joyce's *Ulysses;* she is prosecuted on an obscenity charge and fined $100.

1926 American scientist Robert Goddard makes the first liquid-fueled rocket.

1935 Mao Zedong's 100,000-strong army completes its Long March to Shaanxi. The epic trek covered 6,000 miles and took a year.

the passionate, self-made and self-pickled Klondike golddigger who wrote the gripping animal stories of *The Call of the Wild* (1903) and *White Fang* (1906).

"On or about December 1910," however, the idea had reached England that comfortable Edwardian realism needed some kind of drastic challenge. The words were *Virginia* WOOLF's (1882–1941), speaking of her Bloomsbury friends bringing French modernist painting to London; her own bid to modernize English fiction would head quite otherwise to that of Lawrence, the working-class outsider. A fine-grained insider of the intelligentsia, she further internalized the focus of her nervy, dazzlingly acute prose—onto the so-called "stream of consciousness," events as they pass within the mind. The book that most solidly embodies this airy fluency, locating it among firm familial

D. H. Lawrence.

THE PLOT THICKENS

"Stream of consciousness" (the term comes from **William James**, *Henry's psychologist brother) is a resource many writers draw on, concurrent with Freud—not only Proust and Joyce, but feminist precursors of Woolf like* **May Sinclair** *(1863–1943; e.g.,* The Tree of Heaven, *1917), and* **Dorothy Richardson** *(1873–1957) in her supposedly (hands up, I haven't read it) interminable sequence* Pilgrimage *(1915–57).*

characters, is *To the Lighthouse* (1927; the prose-poetry of *The Waves*, 1931, passes by with the evanescent grandeur of a dream). But what matters more than structure, for many readers, is the new format of sensibility Woolf offers for women's self-consciousness. Those readers are largely based outside England; in her native land, the snobbish streak in her writing has always tangled with English class antagonisms.

Adeline Virginia. "Thinking is my fighting."

Short story

Friend to Lawrence, rival to Woolf: Katherine Mansfield (1888–1923), in the 15 years between leaving her native New Zealand and dying of TB under the roof of the Georgian guru Gurdjieff, brought an arresting, vigorous novelty of tone to English writing, upgrading the short story in pieces like *Bliss* (1920) and *The Garden Party* (1922).

1914 George Bernard Shaw publishes a pamphlet exhorting soldiers of all armies to shoot their officers and go home.

1915 Anthony Comstock, secretary for the American Society for the Suppression of Vice and responsible for the destruction of vast amounts of "obscene" literature, dies.

1916 The first fortune cookies are produced in Los Angeles by George Zung.

1919 Mussolini cofounds a revolutionary, nationalistic group called the Fasci di Combattimento, named for the ancient Roman symbol of power, the fasces.

1914~1928
Oh What a Literary War!
Writers at the Front

Rupert Brooke: known in his day as a remarkable beauty. By Augustus John.

Let's look at Europe's great tragic debacle from a purely literary point of view. Not unequivocally a bad thing, British highbrows opine; it dispelled the post-Victorian flaccidity of British verse (see pp. 66–7), as seen in "Georgian" poets like Rupert BROOKE (1887–1915), with their fey pastoralism. (George V had come to the throne in 1910. British lowbrows, be it noted however, still love the patriotism of golden boy Brooke.) It brought out a new, sterner-edged pastoralism in the late-flowering work of Edward THOMAS (1878–1917), written just before his death in action. (Though this distinguished small oeuvre was also coaxed into being by the encouragement of Robert Frost, see p. 88.) Above all, it prompted new poetic manners, to deal with entirely new experiences, in the so-called "war poets."

Wilfred OWEN (1893–1918) usually fronts this gang—partly for the new techniques he brought to bear (assonant and internal rhymes, resembling Hopkins'), partly because this earnest young officer outraged by the butchering of his men, losing his own life a week before the Armistice, presents an exemplary tragic cameo. But it is *Siegfried SASSOON* (1886–1967) who brings Owen's outrage into articulacy, with his own caustic vision of the slaughter. The poet and composer *Ivor GURNEY* (b. 1890), coming to the fray

THE PLOT THICKENS

Great War experiences: **Jaroslav Hasek** *deserted to the Russians and eventually became a Bolshevik.* **Siegfried Sassoon** *made a public anti-war statement and was sent to a mental hospital, where he met* **Wilfrid Owen** *(who was killed in action in 1918).* **Rupert Brooke** *died of blood poisoning on his way to war.*

1920 King Alexander I of Greece dies after being bitten by his monkey.

1928 Olympic swimming champion Johnny Weissmuller retires. Two years later he starts his new career as the screen Tarzan.

Top novel of the First World War

We've had a lot of entries for this one but a clear overall winner has emerged. Step forward, Mr. Jaroslav Hasek of Prague! (Clutching the rails as you do so, to steady yourself.) The judges unanimously agreed that your *Good Soldier Svejk* (1920–23) was the most disrespectful, the most subversively vulgar, in fact the most irrepressibly hilarious dog's-eye view of the powers that be ever to be scrawled out for beer money in a drunkard's dream. And—a worthy runner-up—will Mr. Ford Madox Ford, of various addresses in London and Paris, please collect a special trophy for *Parade's End* (in four parts, 1924–28). Among the judges' reports we note "greatest work of British fiction of its era," "compelling fusion of modernist splintered consciousness and classic organizing intelligence," "halfway between *War and Peace* and *Gravity's Rainbow*" … Ladies, will you please stop that unseemly squabbling in the auditorium! (Both the authors in question were noted bigamists. What this implies for the literary theorization of war fiction is anyone's guess.)

from a pastoral base, still believed the war was on when he died, shell-shocked, in a mental hospital in 1937; while *Isaac ROSENBERG* (1890–1918), with his jaggedly individual Jewish perspective, was easily the most original British voice to be silenced by the bullets.

Add to this rotten waste of lives (no, nothing's "purely literary," of course), the loss to French

poetry—two days before Armistice—of *Guillaume APOLLINAIRE* (1880–1918). The most frenetically modern of literary hustlers—involved in all the Parisian art movements of the day, alongside his friend Picasso—he is also the most exuberant presence on the page, with his adventures in picture-poetry ("calligrammes"), with his wild and picturesque allusiveness and his eroticism; also his wry humor. "Fine days, sweet days—mice of time. / That's my life that you're nibbling away! / Twenty-eight? God, how my birthdays climb / And how the years went I'd hate to say."

Add also—to look at things from the other side—the Austrian *Georg TRAKL* (1887–1914), dying of a cocaine overdose in a field hospital on the front: a quasi-mystical drug freak whose poetry of dislocated beauty and whose career of deranged excess would prefigure much of the extremism of 20th-century literature.

Hollywood attempts to make a movie of Hasek's *Svejk* in 1963.

1915 In *The Birth of a Nation*, a three-hour-long silent epic, D.W. Griffith transforms cinema, using almost every known film-making technique.

1918 U.S. inventor George B. Hansburg patents the pogo stick.

1922 Worldwide boom in radio broadcasting. The number of radio stations in the U.S. rises from 8 to 600.

1912~1930s
Who? Me?
Ids, Egos, and Superegos

Freud makes more sense—or at any rate is more fun—if you think of him not as a scientist, but as one of a gang of European fiction writers furiously demolishing the façades of the soul in the early 20th century, following on in the wake of Dostoyevsky (see p.74). What is an individual, anyway? What holds us together?

Nothing, reckons *Robert MUSIL* (1880–1942), entitling his sprawling, plotless, pitiless panorama of Austria-Hungary's disintegration *The Man without Qualities* (1930–32). Musil's omnivorously curious mind ranges the breadths of Viennese society and reaches into criminal psychology without ever finding any fixity of character, cause, and effect—or of fictional form. The great Italian dramatist and story writer *Luigi PIRANDELLO* (1867–1936)

Pirandello: an Italian playwright in search of a caption.

would tend to sympathize. Here in the real world our identities are unstable and indefinite; only through resort to fictional characters can we hope for a fixed sense of self. Thus spin the paradoxes of *Six Characters in Search of an Author* (1921), *Henry IV* (1922), and other "mere fictions."

The Portuguese poet *Fernando PESSOA* (1888–1935) takes things further. From 1914, he splits his own persona as a published writer into a multiplicity of pseudonyms: "Caeiro," the natural, instinctive lyric poet; "Campos," the futuristic, Whitmanesque prophet; "Reis," the classicist, etc. Astonishingly, each of

A prophetic tale
The first novel about Freudianism: *Confessions of Zeno* (1923) by Joyce's friend Italo Svevo (1861–1928), a wickedly funny, bitterly sad story about quitting smoking, failing with women, and getting led along by psychoanalysts; it was also the first book to prophesy the coming of the atom bomb.

1924 Celluwipe, the first disposable handkerchief, is introduced to the world. The name is changed to Kleenex' Kerchiefs, then to just Kleenex.

1925 A weekly magazine, the *New Yorker*, is founded. It will have a major influence on literature, journalism, and humor in the U.S..

1929 Construction starts on the Empire State Building in New York—the age of the skyscraper begins.

Writer's block? Kafka tries his hand at drawing.

these facets of "the most complex man that ever lived" is a masterful poet in his own right.

Meanwhile, in Spain, the philosopher *Miguel DE UNAMUNO* (1864–1936) sets author against character in *Mist* (1914): "You are my instrument, and will do as I will"; "No, you are simply an agent for the creation of characters like me …"

But the central fixture in all this relativism (half-echoing Einstein's) is the writing of *Franz KAFKA* (1883–1924), born a German-speaking Jew in Prague. Full of emptiness, dogmatically doubtful, Kafka's prose strides onward in pursuit of a security in which it has no faith. This pursuit generally has a nightmarish form—in short parables like *Metamorphosis*

(1912), about Gregor Samsa's awakening as an insect, and in extended novels like *The Trial* (1925), about Joseph K.'s

Kafka's presence is awesome, even in a passport photo. What was he like to meet?

THE PLOT THICKENS

Meanwhile, in Japan (it's a while since we've been there), modern fiction has been emerging in the hands of two skeptical, quizzical intelligences: **Natsume Soseki** *(1867–1916), dismantling his own identity wittily in* I Am a Cat *(1906), tragically in* The Heart *(or Kokoro, 1914). And* **Junichiro Tanizaki** *(1886–1965), a master who makes sadomasochism and fetishism into the stuff of high art in novels like* A Fool's Love *(1925). In Brazil (this must be our first call— sorry we're a little late), the rise of Latin American literature to world prominence (see p. 124) starts with* Epitaph of a Small Winner *(1880), the hilarious, but nihilistically subversive, dead man's memoirs recounted by* **Machado de Assis** *(1839–1908)— who had clearly been taking a crash course in the works of* **Lawrence Sterne** *(see p. 39).*

---

arraignment for an unknown crime, and *The Castle* (1926). The strange generosity of Kafka is that his muscular writing always opens out on many levels at once— as a prefiguration of the experience of totalitarianism (or, for that matter, of going on welfare), as an echo of our relations with God and death, as a writer musing on the nature of his craft—and yet it can never be reduced to any one of these.

1913~1940

Modern (i.e., Difficult)

Poetic Innovators

Perhaps you can't understand what they're talking about in modernist writing because the modern reality they're trying to represent is like that—incomprehensible. Perhaps it's because you haven't read the right books. Perhaps it's because modernists are portentous poseurs.

Marianne Moore writes *The Pangolin*.

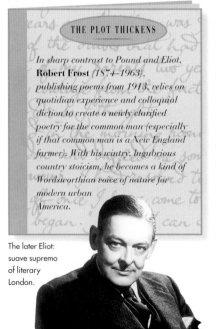

THE PLOT THICKENS

In sharp contrast to Pound and Eliot, **Robert Frost** *(1874–1963), publishing poems from 1913, relies on quotidian experience and colloquial diction to create a newly clarified poetry for the common man (especially if that common man is a New England farmer). With his wintry, lugubrious country stoicism, he becomes a kind of Wordsworthian voice of nature for modern urban America.*

The later Eliot: suave supremo of literary London.

W ell, all of those, really. The point that *Ezra* POUND (1885–1972) or *T. S. ELIOT* (1885–1965) might have countered with, back around 1920, is that there's such a weight of reality on our shoulders at this late stage in history, and that weight includes whole libraries full of books ... and we can't simply turn our backs on them, because that would be evasive; but they are more than we can synthesize into simplicity. And so these supereducated Americans, taking the whole cultural heritage of Europe and Asia on their backs, come out with the splintered, scattershot voices of *The Waste Land* (see also p. 90) and the *Cantos*.

Yet Pound *was* a poseur—a sparky literary agitator, whipping up a fervor for innovation on the London literary scene in the 1910s (also whipping Eliot's famous poem into shape, through inspired editing) before decamping to Italy to immerse himself in the interminably rambling *Cantos* and in a damning association with Fascism. And

1930 Evelyn Waugh converts to Roman Catholicism and publishes *Vile Bodies*.

1938 A research team headed by Wallace H. Carothers discovers nylon. The first nylon stockings are marketed the following year.

The later Pound: lending credence to the plea of insanity which Eliot concocted to save him from the gallows for treachery.

Eliot *was* portentous—constructing in his adopted home of London an edifice of haughty critical authority within which to shield his neuroses, before turning to the resources of mystical experience that would fuel his last, great *Four Quartets* (1935–42). But he could also, thanks to some deep internal dynamic, conjure up rhythms and images that adhere to the soul irremovably, along with Yeats, English poetry's greatest 20th-century voice (which doesn't make either of them admirable human beings).

Pound and Eliot lead a host of American poetic innovators, including Pound's friend William Carlos Williams (see p. 118). There is Eliot's would-be emulator in evoking cosmopolitan complexity, *Hart* CRANE (1899–1932), one of American literature's heroic disasters (*White Buildings*, 1926, huge promise; *The Bridge*, 1930, overreaching failure; alcohol; suicide). There is the laconic but disarming *Marianne* MOORE

Imagism
The wish-child of the doctrines of Mallarmé and the incoming translations of Chinese and Japanese poetry (see p. 19), this concentration on brief, resonant "images"—sans logical connection—was pursued by Pound and associates such as "HD" (Hilda Doolittle) during the 1910s.

(1887–1972), with her faintly perverse poetic principle of "syllabics"; and the bawdy, lightly subversive typographical nightmare *e.e.* CUMMINGS (1894–1962). There is—most crucially, for most *letterateurs*—*Wallace* STEVENS (1879–1955), the insurance company chairman who discreetly devoted his free hours to fashioning profoundly self-reflecting, sonorously slippery meditations about art and its relations with reality. (Emphasize that "slippery": yes, difficult.)

Against these, set the classicist conservatism of the Southerners *John Crowe* RANSOM (1888–1974) and *Allen* TATE (1899–1979); yet these too are poets of deep intelligence, producing work of tremendous spare power.

1922 The BBC starts broadcasting to Great Britain. Sir John (later 1st Baron) Reith, Director-General until 1938, defines its commitment "to educate, to entertain, and to inform."

1924 German movie director Erich von Stroheim directs *Greed*, attempting to express in film what realistic novelists were doing in their books; MGM cuts two thirds.

1932 Joseph Roth publishes his masterpiece *The Radetzky March*. His works will be burned by the Nazis in 1933 and he will spend the rest of his life in exile.

1920~1940

Mythtakes
From Dublin to the Cosmos

"Myth" is religion for those who can't take the discipline. Stories that feel deep, and old, and important—but don't actually commit you to anything specific. And God knows, a writer's life can be hard enough without having to bend your knees, confess your sins, and fast, and all that ...

Dreaming in *Finnegans Wake*.

Before he joined the church in 1927, T. S. Eliot was very keen on myth (Arthurian-style) in *The Waste Land* (1922). He reckoned that it gave that poem's convulsive phantasmagoria a structure. He was particularly keen, for the same reasons, on Homeric myth as the backbone to James Joyce's *Ulysses* (also 1922—the two defining works of modernism, in fact). Does this make sense? What's needed to cope with *Ulysses*?

A sense of humor; a relish for the most gloriously lyrical phrasing—over-the-top yet utterly precise—in English prose; an interest in the minutiae of the mind of an ordinary middle-aged man, and

Joyce immortalized, bestriding the streets of Dublin that in life he fled.

of the streets of Dublin on June 16, 1904; a taste for puns and smut; patience, at times, with arid parodies; a willingness to go with the encompassing flow of Joyce's generosity toward his alter ego Stephen Dedalus and toward his creations, advertisement-seller Leopold Bloom and his wife Molly. Me, I skip; the structure can hang. But I admit I am at cross-purposes with Joyce, who brooded intensively in his Paris exile (from 1920) on the possibility of forging a *world* myth. The results eventually appeared in 1939 as *Finnegans Wake*.

> **Mything in action**
> In the wake of Joyce and Eliot, the artist David Jones (1895–1974) relates his First World War experiences to the archetypes of "the Matter of Britain" (see pp. 76–7) in the fitfully eloquent *In Parenthesis* (1937). Meanwhile John Cowper Powys (1872–1963) pens vast, meandering but eminently mythic melodramas such as *A Glastonbury Romance* (1932). His brother T. F. (1875–1953) wrote the rather more incisive Christian allegory *Mr. Weston's Good Wine* (1927).

1934 Cole Porter, U.S. composer and lyricist, writes "Anything Goes": "Good authors, too, who once knew better words/Now only use four-letter words/Writing Prose/Anything goes.'"

1938 "Orson Welles frightens the nation;" H.G. Wells' *The War of the Worlds* is dramatized for radio in the form of news bulletins.

1940 A schoolboy discovers the Périgord caves, whose paintings show how man lived 16,000 years ago.

The everyday imbued with eternal resonance: myth is central to the art of David Jones.

The pith of myth

Unlike the polyglot, footnote-flirting texts of Joyce, Jones et al., the short poems of Robert Graves (1895–1985) are plain and eloquent English, yet they too looked to a framework of mythology. Graves related them to his saucily idiosyncratic reading of classical and Celtic myth (as set out in *The White Goddess*, 1948), this reading being in turn related to his traumatic love affair with the megalomaniac (if gifted) American poet Laura Riding (1901–91). He once said that "to be a poet is a condition rather than a profession." Besides writing some of the finest love lyrics of the century, Graves unforgettably summed up a generation's reaction to the First World War in the autobiographical *Goodbye to All That* (1929) and opened up classical times in another manner in the large-scale historical novels *I, Claudius* and *Claudius the God* (1934).

Dublin publican Humphrey Chimpden Earwicker sleeps, and the world (and his wife) come to him in a dream. He becomes Gaelic hero Finn MacCool, and his wife Anna Livia is all women, and also the Liffey and all rivers, and their sons are all of vying humanity, and everything is everything, because this is a book written in all languages at once—by a wild and reckless machinery of overloaded puns. Strangely, this total submersion in global information gives the reading of it a waking dream's giddy, giggly shallowness … yet, undeniably, it is an awesome singularity, one of the most ambitious things ever done with words: utterly unique.

Well, not totally unique, actually: the French poets *Paul Claudel* (1868–1955) and Saint-John Perse were aiming for a similarly cosmic perspective in their prose-poems of the 1910s and 1920s. Claudel, imbued with a mystical catholicism, took on the world and tried to glorify it, vaguely Walt Whitman-fashion: following him, SJP set the archetypal wanderings of his *Anabase* (1924) in a heterogeneous world-territory, fusing mythologies in a muzzy grandeur.

1920 In the U.S., the manufacture, sale, and transportation of alcoholic beverages is prohibited. Bootlegging, speakeasies, and smuggling flourish.

1923 Joseph "Buster" Keaton appears in *Our Hospitality*, his first movie in Hollywood.

1924 Harry Houdini, Hungarian-born magician and escapologist, publishes *A Magician Among the Spirits*, an exposé of noted mediums.

1920~1935

Not to Mention Josephine Baker . . .
Gay Paree

Ah, Paris, les années vingt! The réception chez Gertrude[1], and then the taxi to the Ballet Russe for the new Cocteau[2] piece—the lights glittering on the Seine, tu te souviens, mon vieux?—but of course, you caught sight of Pablo and jumped out to join those crazy Surrealist[3] friends of his. Pinning donkey-tails to gendarmes ... ah, vraiment fous. Me, I returned to the Ritz[4] alone, un peu triste ...

Gertrude with fellow artistic poseur Lord Berners.

Gertrude (1). Believed to be a reference to *G. STEIN* (1874–1946), large American resident in Paris from 1902, given to penning prose of a peculiar self-aggrandizing and quickly tiresome drolerie (notably *The Making of Americans*, 1925) and to hosting large droves of visiting literary compatriots. (2) *COCTEAU*, Jean C. (1889–1963), faintly spurious French cultural panjandrum, ubiquitous in this context; good party value. (3) Surrealism.

Doctrinal affiliation propounding the destabilization of civilization via eructation of disjecta from the subconscious mind (i.e., trying to stir it up by putting out antiart art, nonsense poems, wacky public provocations). Novices should address themselves to *André BRETON* (1896–1966), "Pope of Surrealism," author of *Nadja*. Cardinals: his fellow poets Louis Aragon, Paul Eluard, René Char, among a host of figureheads of interwar French culture.

> **MEMO**
>
> At the other end of the Mediterranean, in Alexandria, the Greek Constantine Cavafy (1863–1933) composes a body of tenderly sensual, wistfully civilized lyrics, lamenting past loves and passing civilizations.

1926 Josephine Baker opens her own Paris nightclub at age 20. She rose to fame in the *Folies Bergère*, where she appeared in a g-string decorated with bananas.

1927 Georges Lemaitre, using Einstein's equations, devises the Big Bang theory that the universe is expanding from an explosive moment of creation.

1933 The Reichstag fire gives Chancellor Adolf Hitler the chance to outlaw the Communist party. The Enabling Act gives him four years of dictatorial powers.

Antecedents: Lautréamont (see p. 65), Apollinaire, the Romanian-born poet Tristan Tzara with his nihilistic noncreed of *dada*, reacting to the madness of World War I. Surrealism was the "ism" to end all "isms"—those frantically politicized artistic cabals that dominated the earlier 20th century, though also around at the time there was Imagism (see p. 89), Hermeticism (see box), etc.

(4) Ritz. Location favored by moneyed Americans such as *F. Scott FITZGERALD* (1896–1940) and his wife Zelda: he made the money, and helped her spend it, then he wrote about the process, with an enticing, insider/outsider edge of suave romance and alert disillusionment—in such style as to define the 20s for those living through them. The "Jazz Age" (a term of his own coinage) would be lastingly encapsulated in *The Great Gatsby* (1925), a beautifully poised short fable of excess; thereafter, the times started to roll over him, as Zelda lost her reason and he struggled with the bottle, in one of the classic American literary "crack-ups." (A process given tortuous shape in the lengthy *Tender Is the Night*, 1934, which he believed to be his best novel.) He moved to Hollywood to work as a screenwriter and his flawed final novel, *The Last Tycoon* (1941), was published posthumously.

The Great Gatsby as turned over by Hollywood; directed by Jack Clayton, 1973.

Hermeticism

Label stuck on a bunch of Italian poets who kept their words tightly, "hermetically" sealed against trite interpretations (i.e., by Fascist censors). This doesn't mean they aren't readable—far from it: Giuseppe Ungaretti (1888–1970) is the most persuasive and lyrical exponent of the big white page/ with almost no lines/ and those very short/ type of 20th-century poetry; while Eugenio Montale (1896) transmutes the Mediterranean landscape into beautiful emblems of love and stoic disenchantment.

1918 British women get the vote for the first time.

1920 Dorothy Parker writes the advertising slogan "Brevity is the soul of lingerie."

1923 P.G. Wodehouse publishes *Very Good Jeeves*, featuring Bertie Wooster and his long-suffering butler.

1928 In Italy, Mussolini pronounces that it is unhygienic to shake hands.

1918~1939

Desperately Witty
Huxley, Waugh, and the Women

You are a woman. (At any rate, it's a fifty–fifty chance.) How should you feel about this interesting fact? Fiction of the 1920s and 30s—an age when the mobility of gender roles accelerates—suggests numerous answers. We've already noted the feminist stream-of-consciousness explored by Sinclair, Richardson, and Woolf (see p. 83); then there's the potential of your intuition and sensuality, as presented enticingly in the novels of COLETTE *(1873–1954), e.g.,* Chéri *(1920), and the erotica of Anaïs* NIN *(1903–77); or you could ride the crest of the Jazz Age, as in the giddy stories of Anita Loos or the bons mots of Dorothy Parker; or you could view your disappointments with the male species through the spectacles of Rosamond* LEHMANN *(1901–90), as in* The Weather in the Streets; *or plumb a deeper vein of melancholy in* Good Morning, Midnight *(1939), a high point in the start–stop career of Jean* RHYS *(1890–1979). Among many other alternatives …*

Hard looks from Aldous (probably stemming from his poor eyesight).

MEMO

A Passage to India (1924), E. M. Forster's last novel (though he would live another 46 years), lives on a different scale to his other novels (see p. 77). Opening out from Anglo-Indian social comedy to explore a tragedy of misunderstanding with political and even mystical dimensions, it looks beyond the self-involved Englishness of his earlier work.

The times are changing fast for everyone: and everyone knows it. Invent a new style to cope with the modern, look snappy, be witty if you can. In Britain, Wyndham Lewis writes steely satires of a mechanical society, like *Tarr* (1918); Aldous Huxley flatters even as he ridicules, in romans à clef such as *Crome Yellow* (1921). In their wake, the sharpest comic stylist of all arrives with *Decline and Fall* (1928), the debut of Evelyn WAUGH (1903–66). Waugh's impeccable eye for the ludicrous and his bracingly ruthless reduction of characters to caricatures strike home yet more

1935 W. C. Fields plays Mr Micawber in the movie version of *David Copperfield*.

1939 Grandma Moses' paintings are displayed at New York's Museum of Modern Art. She was 78 when she started painting.

keenly in *Vile Bodies* (1930). But scratch the glittering surface of Huxley's and Waugh's prose and you find a state of desperate cultural anxiety: what are the principles that will underpin us, in this rootlessness that the Great War has left in its wake? Huxley remains through the 1930s in the prolonged adolescence of intellectual dither explored in his greatest novel, *Eyeless in Gaza* (1936). On the way, he leaves off reporting the mindset of the smart set to project a future dystopia in *Brave New World* (1934). The novel is much indebted to the Russian scientist-writer Yevgeny Zamyatin, whose *We* is a brilliantly conceived philosophic satire on Bolshevism.

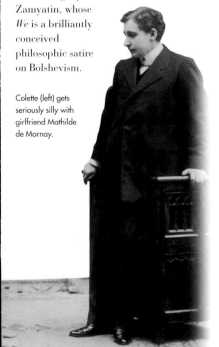

Colette (left) gets seriously silly with girlfriend Mathilde de Mornay.

THE PLOT THICKENS

The most far-reachingly imaginative work of British fiction between the wars: First and Last Men *(1930) by* **Olaf Stapledon**, *a visionary history of future humanity through mutations spanning millions of years; one of the foundational classics of science fiction. The other major figure in the genre at this time—a philosophic satirist, like* **Yevgeny Zamyatin**—*is the Czech* **Karel Capek**—*the original inventor of the "robot" (see* Rossum's Universal Robots, *1921). Capek also wrote several Wellsian utopias, e.g.,* War with the Newts *(1936).*

Waugh, however, like many writers of his generation, opts for a Catholic faith which would increasingly come to the fore in his later novels. A source of stability, but not necessarily an easy option: compare the work of France's greatest novelist of the period, *François MAURIAC* (1885–1970). In *Thérèse* (1927) and *Le Noeud de vipères* (1932) we are away from frenetic modernity, back in the provincial peasant concerns of the Bordeaux region. But we are face to face with the harshest constants of the human soul—possessiveness, fear, and vengeance, and our relations with the God who planted them in us. Mauriac's stern Catholicism sets the scale for personal tragedies of a dignity rarely seen in 20th-century writing.

1917 Nikolai Lenin returns to Russia from Switzerland in a sealed train. Later in the year, the Bolsheviks seize power.

1921 Czech brothers Karel and Josef Capek write *The Insect Play*, an allegorical drama prophesying totalitarianism.

1925 *The Battleship Potemkin*, pioneering Russian movie director Sergei Eisenstein's masterpiece, is released.

1915~1940

In the Kremlin's Shadow
Keeping In with Uncle Joe

Once again (repeating the excursion of p. 62), we head east—to a world on a larger and more alarming scale. Until glasnost, *writing mattered in Russia, in a way that it didn't in more open societies. In St. Petersburg and Moscow, the citadels of intrigue and intellectuality commanding the Empire's communications, there was from the time of Pushkin an intense alternation of fear and admiration between rulers and writers.*

Stalin calls for a chat with Pasternak.

For it was writers who paved the way for the 1917 Revolution: *Maxim* GORKY (1868–1936), penning passionately felt, angry stories about the "lower depths" of the Tsar's realm, helped to create the emotional atmosphere in which it was initially welcomed. Lenin would befriend him, while he in turn would fall in with the repressive tide of Stalin's "socialist realism" come 1932. On a very different level, the poet *Aleksandr* BLOK (1880–1921) spoke for the millennarian hopes of the intelligentsia, as did *Andrei* BELY (1880–1934) in the symbolistic, satiric prose

of *St. Petersburg* (1913–16), one of those modernist novels (compare Dos Passos' *Manhattan Transfer*; see p. 99) in which the city is the hero. Above all, the Bolsheviks could draw strength from the exulting, window-smashing rhythms of Vladimir Mayakovsky—not only the

Kustodiev's stirring image of the palace-storming Bolshevik, 1920.

Socialist realism: Gorky gets jolly with Uncle Joe, 1931.

Futurist of *nash bog byeg,* "our God is speed," but in his love poems, a desperately romantic figure.

But Mayakovsky shot himself on April 14, 1930. A very unsocialist act. As the tyranny rigidified, his romantic postures had become no more than that—postures, parodies of himself. Yet ironically, five years later, after an appeal from his mistress, Stalin exhumed his memory from ignominy to make him official, school textbook poet laureate of the Revolution: total parody. The dictator played with poets the way he played with populations. He phoned *Boris Pasternak* (1890–1960) to ask Pasternak's opinion of *Osip Mandelshtam* (1892–1941). Thrown, Pasternak muffed his lines. "I could have helped my friends better than that," said Stalin, sending Mandelshtam to Siberia. His offense? A circumspect tease of "the Kremlin mountaineer," coming from a poet dedicated not to satire but to a classicist purity of phrase and image that has

made him a model to subsequent poets around the world.

Pasternak, meanwhile—at his best a magically persuasive lyricist—trod a tortuous path as he prepared his famed and only novel, *Dr. Zhivago*—a story of doomed love, set against the Revolution, whose Russian publication he would never see. Like *Anna Akhmatova* (1889–1966), Mandelshtam's fellow in "Acmeist poetry," he was at once accredited as a writer and precluded from publication. Akhmatova, giving shape to the experience of the 1930s purges in *Requiem*, is the central voice of a terrible age. *Marina Tsvetayeva* (1892–1941), with her skittering, conflicting impulses, is its most startlingly individual.

The Master

Though he had once been a favorite of Stalin's, Mikhail Bulgakov thought it prudent to write *The Master and Margarita* (1928–40) in secret. The exuberant, outrageous, and poetic narrative centers on a visit paid by the Devil and his cohorts to the Moscow of writer's clubs and bureaucrats; it parallels this with an inside account of the Passion story, giving a sardonic gloss on the theme of worldly power and the imagination.

1918 The Native American Church is founded. It combines Christian and Native American beliefs.

1923 More than half of the cars in the world are Model T Fords. Ford has produced ten million cars.

1927 Babe Ruth hits a record 60 home runs in a season for the New York Yankees.

1918~1940s
100% American
The Great American Novel

O, to represent America ... Who thought up that all-purpose, overweening ambition—the one that would lead to the eternal quest for the GAN, the "Great American Novel?"

Maybe *Theodore Dreiser* (1871–1945) had something to do with it. Back in 1900, his *Sister Carrie* had brought Americans a new, joltingly raw picture of their urban life; 25 years later, *An American Tragedy* (1925) pitched a claim for brute realism as the means to seize the national essence. (Upton Sinclair, famed for his exposé of the Chicago meatpacking trade in *The Jungle*, 1906, stands on the same side of the argument.)

But there are so many Americas ... and each has its own truth. There is the tough life of Nebraska immigrants, given great moral and artistic dignity in the early novels of *Willa Cather* (1873–1947), such as *My Ántonia* (1918). There is the banality of the Midwest businessman, as satirized with matching banality by *Sinclair Lewis* (1885–1951) in the hugely popular *Babbitt* (1922); there is the world of baseball hopefuls and swindlers in the short stories of the much funnier *Ring Lardner* (1885–1933) (short stories would be big as a literary form in the States, a land much given to magazine reading):

George Babbitt, Midwest real estate agent.

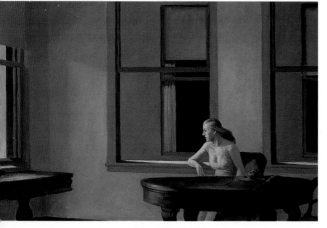

Definitive American angst from Edward Hopper.

1933 Chocolate chip cookies are invented by a Massachusetts woman, Ruth Wade.

1942 Pinball machines are banned in New York because the authorities believe that children are stealing money to play them.

1944 Edmund Wilson, American author and critic, publishes *To the Finland Station*, tracing socialist and revolutionary theory.

Southern sucker: William Faulkner.

and there is, most influentially among fellow writers, the *Winesburg, Ohio* (1919) of *Sherwood ANDERSON* (1876–1941), hitting a vein of authentic, freshly American small-town experience through stylistic precision.

Coming on top of these, there's the self-conscious ambition of *John DOS PASSOS* (1896–1970), wised up on the European moderns and the cinema and applying their techniques to the city of New York in *Manhattan Transfer* (1925). Extending these innovations, he modestly entitles his following trilogy *U.S.A.* (1930–36). Is this the *GAN* it purports to be? No, says the critical consensus; Dos Passos' panoply of facts, figures, and streams of consciousness is all breadth, with no depth.

MEMO

Katherine Anne Porter, an outstanding short story writer, looks beyond local Southern values in her collections *Flowering Judas* (1930) and *Pale Horse Pale Rider* (1939).

When critical opinion concurs in naming a novelist fit to "represent America"—Nobel Prize material, etc.—it swings behind a vision more somber than any of the above: that of *William*

THE PLOT THICKENS

"Southern Gothic" is the label affixed to the grotesquerie, emotional extremism, and sense of tragic doom that pervade not only Faulkner's writing but also that of **Carson McCullers**—*notably* The Heart Is a Lonely Hunter *(1940) and* The Ballad of the Sad Cafe *(1943), her finest short story; it is also to be found in the stories of* **Flannery O'Connor**, *dwelling on social outcasts and on religious desperation. On another level, the romantic pathos of Southern history provided the occasion for one of the century's bestsellers—Margaret Mitchell's only novel,* Gone with the Wind *(1936).*

FAULKNER (1897–1962). On one level, Faulkner's defiantly regional—sticking to his self-created Mississippi land of "Yoknapatawpha County," whose people and past he ranged around from 1929 (*Sartoris*) to 1962 (*The Reivers*). On another, he's an intuitive modernist, spinning extraordinarily varied threads of interior monologue in bold loops around the Southern history that is his organizing concern. But that history is one of violence, defeat, and racial guilt—the abiding human themes in which his status as a "classic" resides. First-rate Faulkner: *The Sound and the Fury* (1929), *As I Lay Dying* (1930), and *Light in August* (1932).

1928 Radclyffe Hall's novel of lesbian love, *The Well of Loneliness*, is condemned in Great Britain and the United States; the American verdict is subsequently reversed.

1929 Imported copies of D. H. Lawrence's *Lady Chatterley's Lover*, published in Florence, are seized and destroyed by order of the British Home Secretary.

1933 Prof. A. M. J. Michels of Amsterdam collaborates with ICI chemists to invent polyethylene.

1920s~1950

Twentieth–Century Fux
(and Macho Goldwyn Mayer)

Of course, pornography bores me ... stiff. But purely in the interests of research, I have gone through John CLELAND's Fanny Hill *(1748), and dipped into Aubrey BEARDSLEY's* Venus and Tannhauser *(1895). It's around the time of the latter, in fact, that the business of representing sex comes forward as a continuous point of literary debate: Hardy and Zola ran into trouble on this score. But the ability to say ***** not to mention ***** * and even to talk about *********!—that's a privilege reserved for the wonderful, liberating century we've just passed through.*

Mindless couplings: Pablo Picasso in surrealist mode in 1931.

Action men
Dressed up in his leather and goggles, Antoine de Saint-Exupéry (1900–44) delights in the freedoms of aerial technology in *Vol de nuit* (1931). (He's also known for the children's book *Le Petit Prince*, 1943.) Drilling a new virility into his erring fellow humans is the soldierly Ernst Jünger (b. 1895), with his earnest parable, *On the Marble Cliffs* (1939). Chasing wars from Shanghai to Spain, the polymathic André Malraux (1901–76)—later to become De Gaulle's right-hand man—is the thinking man's thinker in the thick of things (see *La Condition humaine*, 1933, and *L'Espoir*, 1937).

The failed prosecution of the English publishers of *Lady Chatterley's Lover* in 1959 marks the decisive end of constraints, but D. H. Lawrence had written the book back in 1929. And it was only a few years later that *Henry MILLER*

1948 *The Kinsey Report on Sexual Behavior in the Human Male* is first reviled, then acclaimed; it will be reexamined in the 1990s.

1948 The first issue of *Playboy* magazine appears; Hugh Hefner is its founder, editor, and publisher.

1950 Polygamy ends in China and selling wives is declared illegal.

(1891–1980) went "explicit" in the ebulliently vigorous *Tropic of Cancer* (1934) and its more pretentious successors. Based in Paris (the only place where English readers could then buy *Ulysses*, which they would smuggle across the Channel disguised as Shakespeare's *Works*), Miller linked with Anaïs Nin, a gifted exponent of poetically dressed erotica and of self-fascinated sensibility—who in turn had links with the sex-absorbed Surrealists. Among them was *Georges* BATAILLE (1897–1962), who gave pornography a quasiphilosophical dimension in *Histoire de l'oeil* (1928)—an opening later probed by Pauline Réage (*Histoire d'O*, 1954).

Underlying the new linkage of pen and penis was the impetus that repeatedly affected 20th-century authors: the urge to bring life into writing—to break through everything desiccated, artificial, and aesthetic. Its other major symptom was the rise of the writer as a man of action. Step forward *Ernest* HEMINGWAY (1898–1961): war journalist (Italy in WWI, France in WWII), literary contender (Paris, 1920s), big-game hunter (Africa, early 1930s), soldier (Spanish Civil War), deep-sea fisherman (Cuba, 1950s), all-around tough guy—

> ### THE PLOT THICKENS
>
> *The civil war (1936–39) that drew Hemingway and Malraux to fight with the losing Republican side claimed its most famous victim when Federico* **García Lorca** *(1899–1936) was killed by Fascist troops. A powerful dramatist (e.g. Blood Wedding, 1933), Lorca has also been the best known, most translated poet of modern Spain, with his romantic images of gypsy passion and bullfighting. Many Spaniards consider* **Antonio Machado** *(1875–1939)—no less passionate, but less rhetorical—the finer poet.*

and insistent self-publicist in all these roles. With his terse, macho prose (and pose)—subject-verb-object, cut all the fancy stuff—Hemingway would, from the publication of *The Sun Also Rises* (1926) and *A Farewell to Arms* (1929) onward, act as the definition of modern, matter-of-fact, American writing for many readers. (For a start, he wouldn't write sentences as convoluted as the one you've just read.) It's a style that makes you want to go out and live more, though it's also stuck on a be-all-end-all concern for masculine honor that closes off half the nuances that make life interesting.

Hemingway gets reel in Florida, 1928.

101

1931 Conductor Arturo Toscanini is punched in Rome for refusing to play the Fascist national anthem.

1933 The Teasmade and the anglepoise desk lamp are two of the year's "must-have" home accessories.

1934 Hungarian-born Arthur Koestler, unemployed in Paris, writes *The Encyclopaedia of Sexual Knowledge* under the pseudonym "Dr. A. Costler."

1930s
Fellow Traveling
McSpaunday *et al.*

The dates are still etched on the collective memory. 1929: Wall Street Crash. 1933: Hitler to power. Between them, the world's mood plunges. New writers hitting the scene

Isherwood's Berlin, as seen in *Cabaret*.

at this point face a choice of desperate extremes— Communism; Fascism; a seemingly doomed Old World civilization; the "Fordist" automatized mass capitalism of the U.S.; the refuge of the Church. Very largely, they opt for the first, blinding themselves to the nature of Stalinism. The prospect will grow increasingly dark until the "low, dirty, dishonest decade" ends on September 3, 1939.

Grapes of Wrath

The 1930s Depression in America is lastingly associated in popular memory with one book—*The Grapes of Wrath* (1939), in which John Steinbeck took the Joad family of farm laborers from the dustbowl of Oklahoma to the "promised land" of California. For its part, the name of John Steinbeck is lastingly associated in critical circles with sentimentality and crass simplicity— this despite (or because of?) his vigor as a storyteller, and the international enthusiasm which led to his Nobel Prize in 1962.

The phrase belongs to one of the poems that made *W. H. AUDEN* (1907–73) chief spokesman for his generation in England. Auden is an almost embarrassingly brilliant lyricist— suavely au fait with the poetic rulebook and with the latest trends in Marxism and Freudianism, yet brimming over with quirky imagery and nervous passion.

Guernica, 1937: Picasso's angry response to Hitler's bombing of the town.

Looking back on the 1930s from the security of the U.S., where he based himself from 1939, he would come to repudiate his runaway phrasemaking (notably the notorious condoning of "the

1937 Eric Blair (George Orwell) joins an anarchist unit to fight against the Fascists in the Spanish Civil War. *Homage to Catalonia* will appear in 1938.

1937 Pablo Picasso paints *Guernica*, depicting his native Spain in a terrifying, distorted image.

1939 Russian designer Igor Sikorsky makes a successful flight in his VS-300 helicopter.

necessary murder" in "Spain," his most excited call for political engagement). His English readers, in turn, would regret the loss of fire in his verse as he settled during the 1940s and 1950s into a rueful, temperately religious middle-age manner.

They harked back to the presence, in the mid-1930s, of a literary phenomenon in their midst: the left-leaning composite beast "McSpaunday." This also comprised *Stephen SPENDER* (1909–95), whose reputation as a dedicated Party-joining, party-going trend follower has lasted better than that of his poems; *Cecil DAY LEWIS* (1904–72), also a versatile versifier who would later swing right—ending his days as poet laureate (almost invariably a joke of a job); and *Louis MACNEICE* (1907–63), whose essential decency and technical flair make him, for many, the most attractive of this gang.

THE PLOT THICKENS

César Vallejo *from Peru and* **Pablo Neruda** *from Chile both travel from youths spent in poverty to fight with the Communist Party in Spain. Vallejo, transforming his firsthand experience of the anguish of life into poetry of extraordinary intensity, dies there; Neruda, a winningly immediate love poet and glorifier of his continent's natural beauties, goes on to become international Communism's favorite figurehead and dies in Santiago following the CIA coup against his colleague Allende.*

The McSpaunday moniker omits Auden's chief literary associate (and lover) *Christopher ISHERWOOD* (1904–86)— chiefly famed for his prose portraits of Berlin before Hitler. Isherwood's Berlin of cabarets and con men interfaces with the proletarian city of crooks, whores, and porters rendered in Alfred Döblin's magnum opus *Berlin Alexanderplatz* (1929); the vaudeville world and the reckless desperation of the poor come together in *The Threepenny Opera* (1928), a major landmark in the theatrical career of *Bertolt BRECHT* (1898–1956).

Weaving in and out of allegiance to the Communist Party, unscrupulous, provocative, and systematically scornful, Brecht was also a masterly poet with a great range of feeling, and the left's most vigorous European voice.

1931 Al "Scarface" Capone, most famous of American mobsters, is convicted and imprisoned—for income tax evasion.

1934 The film industry publishes its new Production Code to protect audiences from seeing the excesses of moral depravity on screen.

1938 Superman and Batman make their debuts in the same year, stopping evil villains from achieving world domination.

1930 ~ 1947

Low and Seedy
Crime Thrillers

Popular fiction doesn't need the mantle of "literature"—of high art and cultural dignity; that's what publishers reach for to shift work that makes greater demands on the concentration. But "literature" needs repeatedly to reach for the power and appeal of popular fiction if it is to retain its vitality.

It probably mattered little to superb crime writers like *Georges SIMENON* (1903–89) or *Margery ALLINGHAM* (1904–66)—or the phenomenally efficient *Agatha CHRISTIE* (1890–1976)—whether or not their well-honed art of plotting, psychology, and atmosphere was saluted as capital-L "literature." But in the 1930s, with the great age of modernism past and

THE PLOT THICKENS

As with many British novelists, the national class system served as material for **Henry Green** *(1905–73)—but material that he played with in a singular spirit of tender detachment and fascinated artistry. Closely observing the passions and speech of both moneyed society* (Party Going, *1939) and working-class people* (Loving, *1945), he constructed tantalizing, self-conscious singularities: modernist art sniffing its way around the factual world.*

political and class concerns to the fore, a self-conscious young writer like *Graham GREENE* (1904–91) headed straight for the detective and thriller genres in *Stamboul Train* (1932) and *Brighton Rock* (1938). Greene, lured by both Catholic and left-wing ideals, went on to write a long series of tales of suspense, sin, and betrayal, usually exotic in setting—e.g. Mexico for *The Power and the Glory* (1940), Vietnam for *The Quiet American* (1955)—and always accessible in style. But with *Brighton Rock* he touches on the territory of moral/physical/social sleaze— "seediness"—that he seems to rediscover in every location.

Mexico. Mauve mountains and mescal. The destination for English writers Graham Greene and Malcolm Lowry and setting for powerful novels from each.

1943 A District of Columbia Court indicts Ezra Pound for treason, after a jury finds him of "unsound mind."

1944 British artist Francis Bacon paints *Three Studies of Figures for the Base of a Crucifix*, combining disturbing and repulsive elements.

1947 Thor Heyerdahl sails the balsa-wood raft *Kon-tiki* from Peru to Polynesia.

The Maltese Falcon, filmed in 1941, with Humphrey Bogart, Peter Lorre, Gladys George, and Sydney Greenstreet.

Paperbacks

The 1930s sees the advent in Britain of the cheap mass-market novel—with the launch of Penguin Books in 1935, a major factor in bringing together "high" literature and "low" genres in a democracy of writing. The American equivalent, Pocket Books, hits a market earlier dominated by book clubs in 1939.

That territory of sordid, sweaty compromise and corruption preoccupies many of the period's sharpest portraitists. Patrick Hamilton's *Hangover Square* (1941) is a particularly fine example of the genre film critics would later call *noir*; the early novels of George Orwell likewise wallow in the petty grunge of modern living conditions. Thriller writers, working the psychology of fear and betrayal—e.g. the masterly Eric Ambler and Geoffrey Household, author of *Rogue Male* (1939)—also thrive during the 1930s. But the central text in all this turn toward squalor—which is also a sort of turn toward "real life" (see p. 100)—comes from France: *Voyage au bout de la nuit* (1932), the first novel of Louis-Ferdinand Céline. A gross,

Mr. Hardboiled

Dashiell Hammett (1894–1961), developing on his experiences as a San Francisco private dick in novels like *The Maltese Falcon* (1930) and *The Glass Key* (1931), makes the streamlined, businesslike, fact-nagging toughness of crime writing into a kind of moral virtue—though there's nothing virtuous about the world he depicts.

grotesque, partly allegorical tirade against Europe in the wake of World War I, it hits base when it sets its doctor protagonist among the decaying bodies of the urban poor, and lets rip in unrestrained scum-sucking street invective.

Later books damningly exposed Céline's fascistic anti-Semitism. Yet he sets a prototype for writing as a purge, a harrowing-of-the-hell that is modern civilization. Witness, above all, the solitary masterwork of Malcolm Lowry—*Under the Volcano* (1947), set, like *The Power and the Glory*, in Mexico and in a morass of alcohol. Under a looming smolder of mythic and literary archetypes, Firmin, Lowry's mescal-sodden fictional persona, confronts his own imminent extinction, and that of his culture: the story is set in 1939.

1942 American humorist James Thurber's short story "The Secret Life of Walter Mitty" appears in the *New Yorker*.

1943 Germans suppress a revolt by Polish Jews. The Warsaw ghetto is destroyed.

1943 Swiss chemist Albert Hofmann, investigating the ergot fungus, accidentally discovers LSD.

1940~1950s

The Usefulness of Typewriters
Social Conscience

George ORWELL *(1903–50) is probably the most important voice in British writing between the time of the great moderns (Lawrence, Eliot, etc.) and the end of the 20th century. But this isn't, ultimately, due to any creative achievement of his. It is true that* Animal Farm *(1945) is one of the most influential— and beautifully poised—political satires ever written; and that* Nineteen Eighty-Four—*the dystopian counter-image of the 1948 in which it was written—shows a profoundly dark imagination working at a very high level.*

George hits the airwaves, 1945.

But the lasting presence of Orwell in British culture is that of a conscience that sets imagination in its place—below that of "decency," the fuzzy attractive value that makes everyone, from anarchists to conservatives, want to claim Orwell for their own. The voice speaking up for it uses fiction, as it uses journalism. Once again, as with Dr. Johnson (see p. 39), an individual's restraining critical and moral tone would hold the national cultural reins—a mixed blessing, perhaps, for other writers' imaginative self-confidence.

But Orwell's use of fiction for political ends was typical of the 1940s. It echoed the work of the Hungarian-born polymath Arthur Koestler, with his great exposé of Stalinism, *Darkness at Noon* (1940), as well as the work of André Malraux (see p. 100). In the cafés of Paris' Left Bank, the "politically committed writer" was the role in

Francis Bacon's offal triptychs were tailored to existentialist sensibilities.

1945 American planes drop the atom bomb on the Japanese cities of Nagasaki and Hiroshima. The war in the Pacific ends.

1949 Silly Putty—an apparently useless substance that can be molded, stretched, and bounced—is successfully marketed by advertising man Peter C. L. Hodgson as a new toy.

1955 Ruth Ellis is convicted of killing her lover; she will be the last woman in Britain to be hanged.

which Jean-Paul Sartre and his partner Simone de Beauvoir would exult for three decades from the Liberation of 1944—the one pitching for every hard-line position from anticolonialist terrorism to Maoism, the other opening up a political space for feminism. De Beauvoir did this by making a continuity of her personal experience and fiction like *L'Invitée* (1943); Sartre through the panoramically ambitious three-part portrait of his times, *Les Chemins de la liberté* (1945–50).

Nonetheless there remains a space between the politics and the art. Sartre's first and greatest novel, the Surrealistically terrifying *La Nausée* (1938), exists apart from the existentialism (see box) he would make famous; while his cophilosopher and political sparring partner, the more liberal Albert

The Existentialist existence

There's no essential human nature, no earthly role you're bound to fulfill. Your existence is in your own hands—it's up to you to become conscious of this alarming freedom (not like the conformist cabbageheads). Go ahead, choose this consciousness, and acknowledge that it makes you politically responsible to your fellow humans. Acknowledge your political duty to demonstrate, to wear black turtleneck sweaters, to chain-smoke, and to listen to bebop. Dig Bacon and Giacometti. Read Beckett (see p. 112).

Camus, wrote classically freestanding works of art in *L'Étranger* (1942), *La Peste* (1947), and *La Chute* (1956). Transmuting his experience as a "poor white" youth in French Algeria into prose of compelling, nuscular nobility, Camus created inclusive parables: as with Orwell, everyone from left to right of the spectrum would make a grab for premier rights of interpretation. (A manuscript left unfinished by Camus, *Le Premier Homme*, was published 34 years after his death in a car crash in 1960. Some readers think it his finest work.)

The Duchess of Windsor with a prominent mobster? No, it's only Jean-Paul and Simone taking a Paris stroll.

MEMO

Cesare Pavese (1908–50) wrote novels that are broadly in the "neorealist" mode favored by the other great Italian novelist of the postwar generation, Alberto Moravia (see p. 115). Their tragic aspect was underlined when Pavese killed himself following completion of the finest, *The Moon and the Bonfires* (1950).

1946 Timex watches are launched at $6.95 each. During the war, their Norwegian-American creator, Joakim Lehmkuhl, had made timing mechanisms for bombs.

1947 Bertolt Brecht's drama *Galileo* is produced in Hollywood by Charles Laughton.

1948 T. S. Eliot publishes Robert Graves' *The White Goddess*. Two other publishers have rejected it; both die shortly afterward.

1937~1950s
That's Strange . . .
From Fantasy to Sci-fi

Tolkien's Gollum with the eponymous Ring.

Storytelling: modernism thinks it's a little unsound ("Oh dear yes, the novel tells a story"—E. M. FORSTER, 1927), 20th-century realism labors hard to make it plausible—and a whole other strand of writing doesn't give a damn about everyday probability, because it simply loves a good story!

Yes, we're talking about fantasy—but not quite that alone. The screeds of *Hermann HESSE* (1877–1962), I guess, are fantasy—at any rate, folks on my street don't go loopily lupine like they do in *Steppenwolf* (1927)—but good storytelling they aren't. (In fact, why anyone accords this weakly written pseudomysticism the status of "modern classic" is beyond me.) Although the superb *Seven Gothic Tales* (1935) of *Isak DINESEN* (that's really Karen Blixen, 1885–1962, famed for her memoir *Out of Africa*, 1937) don't actually exceed the possibilities of their 19th-century settings, they do transmute them into something rich and strange.

Strangeness—that's half the essence of storytelling; to be taken to another plane, charmed by it, chilled. It's for the sake of strangeness that *J. R. R. TOLKIEN* (1892–1973) had to map himself out a whole alternative universe in which to enact his massively ramified, brilliantly imaged grand

The romantic, young (prebooze) Dylan Thomas painted by the old (postbooze) Augustus John.

1950 Raymond Chandler's essay "The Simple Art of Murder" stabs the British detective tale to the heart.

1952 Agatha Christie's play *The Mouse Trap* opens in London; amazingly, it is still running in 1998.

1955 Modern scientific methods applied to the allegedly ancient remains of Piltdown Man reveal an archaeological fraud.

narration, *The Lord of the Rings* (1954–55). It's a shame that with the pacy success of *The Hobbit* (1937) behind him he felt encouraged to wallow in such flaccid, overblown prose—but he was being egged on by a highly articulate advocate of narrative as against modernism, his friend *C. S. LEWIS* (1898–1963).

Both these Oxford dons (like Lewis Carroll) directed their imaginations toward the children's book market, but their word carried a clout beyond it in 1940s and 1950s Britain. That sobersided culture needed to express imagination somehow; other outlets were the Arthurian novels of *T. H. WHITE* (*The Once and Future King*, 1938–58) and the massive, somber masonry of Mervyn Peake's *Gormenghast* trilogy (1946–59), with its lugubrious, fantastical humor and gargantuan structure.

In the U.S., meanwhile, equal energy was going into the growth of the science-fiction market—mainly through magazine stories. In this "Golden Age" of science fiction, dry, ingenious extrapolations of future worlds, like those of *Isaac ASIMOV* (1920–92) (*The Foundation Trilogy*, 1951–53), rubbed shoulders with the picturesque, whimsical

Tolkien, "Master of Middle Earth," posing as an affable Oxford don.

writing of *Ray BRADBURY* (b. 1920) (*The Silver Locusts*, 1950), while the polished, provocative stories of Theodore Sturgeon (e.g. *More Than Human*, 1953) make more of a nod in the direction of literary "good taste." (The spectrum of 1950s British science fiction would run from Arthur C. Clarke to John Wyndham, with his alien disturbances in middle England. See p. 123 for the American experience.)

THE PLOT THICKENS

At Swim-Two-Birds (1939) is one of the great antinovel novels—about a man writing a book about writing a book about ... Its real author, **Flann O'Brien** *(1911–66; or 'Myles na Gopaleen' in his wonderful journalism), an Irish experimentalist a generation after Joyce, offers a wealth of verbal felicity and humor (satiric or just plain ludicrous) that's virtually matchless—though an undercurrent of deep, sardonic fatalism shows in the wildly contrasting* The Third Policeman *(1940) and* The Poor Mouth *(1941).*

1943 The first electronic digital computer, Colossus, is developed in Britain to break German codes.

1945 Charlie "Bird" Parker and Dizzy Gillespie make the first bebop recordings.

1946 Humphrey Bogart appears as Chandler's world-weary private eye, Philip Marlowe, in *The Big Sleep*.

1940s~1963
So Stylish It Hurts
Chandler, Nabokov, and Bellow

James Baldwin, son of a preacher, writes on racial issues and homosexuality.

People often say that Raymond CHANDLER (1888–1959) is a great "stylist." "Stylist?"— Hmmmm. Would that mean surface not substance, flash not flesh? That isn't the case with Chandler. His best novels, like The Little Sister *(1949), revel in the awkwardness of life as lived by private dick Philip Marlowe; the hard-stretched plots swallow many hangovers' worth of intrusive reality. But the general implication is, all life's grit will turn to jewels of wit if you grind your prose hard enough: O.K., that's style.*

That's the premise on which L.A.'s greatest alcoholic hack concurs with the émigré aristocrat who exotically descended on American culture in the 1940s. After a run of fey, ingenious novels in Russian and then English, *Vladimir NABOKOV* (1899–1977) achieved nationwide notoriety in 1955. *Lolita* turned his kid-gloved, tightly smiling curiosity toward the world of motels and gas stations—but focused it around an aesthetic fantasist's obsession for a pubescent girl. Seducing her, "Humbert Humbert" fatally transgresses the line between style and life—such was the "moral" theme critics brought forward to defend the book against outraged sexual

Hammett's heirs

Ross MacDonald (b. 1915) took up the private detective territory opened up by Dashiell Hammett— to be followed by a thousand other purveyors of hard-boiled style. Outstanding among their number during the 1970s and 1980s: Ed McBain, Elmore Leonard, Walter Mosley, and Sara Paretsky.

1950 George Bernard Shaw, Irish dramatist, essayist, socialist, and wit dies, aged 94, after suffering a broken hip.

1951 Ludwig Wittgenstein, one of the most original and influential philosophers of the 20th century, dies.

1963 Scandal rocks the British government. John Profumo, secretary of war, is found to have lied about his sexual relationship with a call girl.

moralists. Yet Nabokov himself remained the great exemplar of literary poise and panache—never more so than in *Pale Fire* (1962), consisting of a 400-line poem with annotations by an academic who slowly reveals how he murdered the poet.

Postwar American culture needed style masters like Chandler and Nabokov, each fashioning a tone with which to negotiate its complex, fast-shifting urban life—a choice of ways to feel good about walking down the street. From a quite different direction, it got another in *Saul BELLOW* (b. 1915). Garrulous, querulous, hitting every which way with streetwise, abrasive phrasing, Bellow's individualist spokesmen from Chicago Jewry make grabs for the essence of contemporary cultural dilemmas. The manner established in *The Adventures of Augie March* (1953) and epitomized in *Herzog* (1964) is not just a style, however; it aims to speak up for what it is to be a man—as against everything

> ### THE PLOT THICKENS
>
> *For Americans being tough, hard-headed, and honest about life see* Native Son *(1940),* **Richard Wright's** *tragedy of an African American outsider. For individualists seeking symbolic meaning see* Invisible Man *(1952),* **Ralph Ellison's** *virtuoso, dexterously symbolical performance on the same theme of African American alienation. Third in this lineage of consciousness raisers is* **James Baldwin,** *whose writing after the autobiographical* Go Tell It on the Mountain *(1953) shuttles racial issues with those of sexual orientation.*

that dehumanizes us in our man-made world. (Though wouldn't it speak better if it spoke less?)

Bellow was one of a group of Jewish writers who moved to center stage in the northeastern literary scene of the 1950s; others were Bernard Malamud, meditating on the nature of Jewishness in *The Assistant* (1957); Philip Roth (see p. 121); also—translated from his native Yiddish by Bellow—Isaac Bashevis Singer, whose richly humane stories brought back life to the destroyed *shtetls* of Eastern Europe. American literature—already rich in regional manners—was diversifying into ethnic traditions.

James Mason as Humbert Humbert and Sue Lyon in the title role: Stanley Kubrick's 1962 *Lolita*.

1950 The birth control pill is developed.

1951 Julius and Ethel Rosenberg, accused of passing information about the atomic bomb to Soviet agents, are the first U.S. civilians to be executed for espionage.

1952 Moviemaker Alfred Hitchcock directs the spine-chiller *Psycho*.

1950~1970

Look, Real Blood
Voices from the Edge

Committed individuals, on the cutting edge of experience—tough, extreme, even maimed—that was what Existentialism (see p. 107) seemed to call for.

Top of its literary pantheon had to be the aquiline, taciturn figure of *Samuel BECKETT* (1906–89), Joyce's designated successor as Irish modernist maestro, of whose ever sparser utterances Paris stood in awe from *Waiting for Godot* onward (1953; it was first done in French, like most of his stuff). Formidable reputation aside, Beckett can be an incredibly funny writer, generously throwing out delicious phrasings (see his early novels, e.g. *Murphy*, 1938)—but all his writing heads back to the edge where words stop and

what can't be spoken of (which might be reality; might be non-existence) begins. Like Kafka's, it is steelily single-minded and awesomely empty-handed. Poetry on a comparable edge of utterability came from *Paul CELAN* (1920–70), a German-speaking Jew who glanced on his virtually incommunicable experience of the "Final Solution" with terrible power in "Fugue of Death," and who would go on to end his own life.

Another "saint" of Existentialism (in Sartre's designation) was *Jean GENET* (1910–86), thief, male prostitute, rhapsodic prose-poet of *Notre-Dame-des-fleurs* (1943), in which he glorified this outsider existence.

This ethos of personal extremism hit American writing in the later 1950s. It met two of the strongest-

Mishima

Like Kleist (see p. 44), the Japanese Yukio Mishima was a storyteller who seemed determined to make a story out of his own life by ending it spectacularly. After the success of his harsh, brilliant tales of revenge and homosexuality (e.g. *The Sailor Who Fell from Grace with the Sea*, 1963), he stormed an army HQ with a gang of fascist followers, calling for abandonment of Japan's pacifism, then ritually disemboweled himself.

Beckett directing the German actor Martin Held.

1958 Bertrand Russell founds the Campaign for Nuclear Disarmament (CND) in Great Britain.

1960 69 black Africans are killed and 180 injured in the Sharpeville Massacre in South Africa when police open fire on a crowd protesting at the oppressive pass laws.

1961 Suicide ceases to be defined as a crime in Great Britain.

voiced poets of the past decade, *Robert Lowell* (1917–77) and *John Berryman* (1914–72), each coming from a tight and grim engagement with Catholic religion: it teamed up with the vogue for psychoanalysis and took them off on a spree of self-exploration, cracking apart the hard-wrought surfaces of their earlier verse and letting loose the viscera beneath … The resulting "confessional" verse has been controversial ever since. In Berryman's case it seems to fall in with the natural drift of his woebegone drunkard's persona: in Lowell's, there's a sneaking feeling that it belongs to a career dedicated to enacting whatever America's current idea of "the great poet" was (even if he did genuinely skirt madness).

Its most striking products came from Anne Sexton and *Sylvia Plath* (1932–63), each seeming to splash fresh blood on the page with jagged stabs of recklessly self-lacerating verse.

Plath, in fact, was a writer with more wit and breadth than this description might suggest; but her work has become permanently snarled up in the fame of her suicide. Which has also, ever since, entangled her husband *Ted Hughes* (1930–98)—the fiercest and most original poetic voice in 1950s Britain.

MEMO

Working traditional verse forms with great elegance, Thom Gunn gave youth angst a sharply intellectual voice in *Fighting Terms* (1954) before moving on to California and the terrain of gay culture.

English boyhood reverts to barbarity in Golding's *Lord of the Flies*, filmed in 1990. The novel was an immediate success on publication in 1954.

THE PLOT THICKENS

Wielding a determined, tough-skinned prose, **William Golding** *moved through adventure stories* (Lord of the Flies, *1954), quasi-science fiction* (The Inheritors, *1955), and fantasy parables* (Pincher Martin, *1956) to pare open humanity's emptiness and flawed, evil heart. (His writing's more confused, but arguably richer, in the later* Darkness Visible, *1979.)*

1950 Cartoonist Charles M. Schulz creates *Peanuts*, the most commercially successful comic strip of its time.

1955 Scandinavian designers turn their attention to stainless steel tableware, which is to prove popular across Europe.

1956 When President Nasser nationalizes the Suez Canal, Anglo-French forces invade Egypt but withdraw after the U.S. protests.

1950s~1960s

Realism, Again. Really?
Novels from Hot Countries

So what happened to realism? All that mid-19th-century getting to grips with the fabric of social existence—Madame Bovary, Middlemarch, War and Peace—*did it just evaporate? No, a hundred years later it was alive and well, but living at a different address.*

The India experience in *Heat and Dust.*

In Arabic literature, where novel writing only started in the 1910s, Naguib Mahfouz produced a magnificently fully imagined, socially rich—O.K., you could say old-fashioned—portrait of Cairo life in the *Palace Walk* trilogy (1956–58). In southern India, R. K. NARAYAN (b. 1906) created a story town of "Malgudi" as real as Trollope's "Barchester"—but funnier—in novels such as *The Maneater of Malgudi* (1961) or *The Guide* (1958), while the Delhi-based Ruth Prawer JHABVALA (b. 1927) portrayed India and its tensions

Oskar beating *The Tin Drum* from a 1979 movie based on Günter Grass' novel.

THE PLOT THICKENS

The shaking-off of colonialism had to start with hearts and minds—and what better to reach them than poetry? **Aimé Césaire,** *from Martinique in the French West Indies, shaped a voice for Afro-Caribbean experience in* Cahier d'un retour au pays natal *(1939), fusing surrealism with the history of slavery. His friend* **Léopold Senghor,** *raising Césaire's angry negritude to a lofty philosophic vagueness, would become first president of his native Senegal in 1960, a position he held on to for twenty years.*

with the Europe she came from in *Esmond in India* (1958) and successors, including *Heat and Dust* (1975). The African novel in English effectively starts with Chinua Achebe's insider's view of Nigerian village society and

1962 The Beatles make their first recording and the "Swinging Sixties" era commences.

1969 James Fisher's *The Red Book* lists animals and plants threatened with extinction.

1970 New York State legalizes abortion; it is already legal in most Eastern European and Scandinavian countries, Japan, and Great Britain.

colonial intrusion, *Things Fall Apart* (1958). The Kenyan *Ngugi Wa* THIONG'O (b. 1938) also spoke firsthand about the disruption of tribal life (*The River Between*, 1965).

The most famous product of this upsurge of hot-country realism is V. S. Naipaul's deeply comic, pathos-filled portrait of his father's struggle to establish a rooted dignity, as a man of Indian Brahmin stock, in the tropical soil of Trinidad. *A House for Mr. Biswas* (1962) is one of the masterpieces of later 20th-century fiction; it has rather overshadowed the other great novelist of Caribbean life, the Barbadian George Lamming, author of *In the Castle of My Skin* (1953). Lamming, unlike the stoically conservative Naipaul, was fired by political anger; and maybe most of these books can be classed, not so much as European-style realism, but as "consciousness-raising" for new political communities.

Meanwhile, in Europe, "neorealist" was the critical moniker bestowed on *Alberto* MORAVIA (b. 1907); not that this robust,

Renato Guttoso's paintings share the "neorealist" ethos of Moravia's fiction.

Deep in history
The postwar period in Europe also sees several grand, isolated plunges into the historical past, recent and ancient— Hermann Broch's arduous modernist meditation on *The Death of Virgil* (1945); Marguerite Yourcenar's *Memoirs of Hadrian* (1951); Pasternak's *Dr. Zhivago* (see p. 97); and *The Leopard*, the posthumously published solitary masterpiece of the Sicilian prince Giuseppe di Lampedusa, with its rich, ironically romantic portrait of his forebears in the 1860s.

compassionate storyteller needed it in his confrontations with the Fascists (who gagged his earlier writings, like *The Fancy Dress Party*, 1941) and the Vatican (which forbade his later works, like *The Woman of Rome*, 1947, for being too sexy). In Germany, trying to recompose itself after Hitler, social observation really acted as the pretext on which *Heinrich* BÖLL (1917–85) could build his acute analyses of the nation's bad faith, while Günter Grass, in *The Tin Drum* (1959)—a novel whose impact exceeded any other in Adenauer's state—left realism decisively behind. A parable of Nazism told through the grotesque adventures of Oskar—the child who just decides to stop growing up—it presages the "fabulism" of later European fiction. (Find that on pp. 126–27).

1952 Elizabeth II is crowned queen—her reign will witness the dismantling of the British Empire and the decline of the British monarchy.

1956 Rock 'n' roll singer Elvis Presley records "Heartbreak Hotel," his first hit.

1962 American environmentalist Rachel Carson protests about the indiscriminate use of pesticides in her book *Silent Spring*.

1950~1970s

"What Is Happening to Our Culture?"
Larkin, Amis the Elder, and Murdoch

"Sadly, he was half inaudible, short, and fat.
Was this *the man whose senses tingled?"*
Brian Hinton's lines on a poetry reading speak for us all: why aren't the poets we admire more admirable as human beings? Why was Philip Larkin, as revealed posthumously in his letters, such a mean-hearted, masturbatory xenophobe?

H. M. Bateman's *The Wrong People*. Powell's and Amis's novels are full of them.

stanza on the communal memory—from the blunt dourness of "They fuck you up, your mum and dad" (currently the most quoted line in English poetry) to the careful loveliness of "Cut Grass" or "Wedding Wind." The trade-off between his art and his fatalism created some beautiful things. But it is the negativity that lingers.

It does so in the context of an anti-imaginative culture—in the wake of Orwell (see p. 106) and of *F. R. LEAVIS* (1895–1978), the critic who took D. H. Lawrence as a model of modernity that was also *moral*: serious, sober, culturally responsible. Such responsibility hung heavy on postwar British novelists—even if they were comedians like Larkin's friend *Kingsley Amis* (1922–95). The lighthearted social comedy of *Lucky Jim*

The question mattered in 1990s Britain because *LARKIN* (1922–85)—following Yeats, Eliot, and Auden—had become the dominant presence in its poetry. Standing high above the rest of his colleagues in the 1950s grouping of "the Movement," with its emphasis on low-key good craftsmanship, he stamped stanza upon

1963 British spy Kim Philby defects to the USSR. His friends Burgess and Maclean left in 1951. But who is the fourth man?

1964 Geometric designs and violently contrasting colors give the illusion of pulsing light and movement; "Op Art" is born.

1965 British fashion designer Mary Quant popularizes the miniskirt.

THE PLOT THICKENS

Anthony Powell *took it on himself to produce a magnum opus in the 12 novels from* A Question of Upbringing *(1951) to* Hearing Secret Harmonies *(1975)—collectively entitled* A Dance to the Music of Time. *His mellifluously amusing, character-packed, ingeniously woven sequence, tinged with a wistfulness characteristic of postwar British cultural reflection, stands as the major achievement of the period—though it doesn't do to dwell on the comparison it seeks to draw between itself and Proust.*

(1954) took to a curmudgeonly scowl in later novels, leavened by a superb ear for common diction. Likewise, Angus Wilson moved from devastatingly sharp short stories (*Such Darling Dodos*, 1950) to lengthy, labored inquisitions of British culture: the title *No Laughing Matter* (1967) is all too much to the point. Equally earnest about Englishness were the sisters A. S. Byatt—thoughtful but turgid—and Margaret Drabble (whose novels no one reads these days but whom God preserve, for she has edited the indispensable *Oxford Companion to English Literature*). The best focused writing of the period came in the novels of Alan Sillitoe and David Storey, opening up new territories of working-class experience.

Some authors tried to overtake the truckloads of social realism that kept so much British fictional traffic in second gear. Notable among them were William Golding (see p. 113) and *Iris MURDOCH* (b. 1919). Murdoch's mannered arabesques of polymorphous passion and philosophic speculation, taken in some quarters for the most ambitious work of her generation, are an acquired taste this reader has somehow completely failed to acquire. Far wittier and sharper—if rather smaller in scale—are the equally self-conscious and equally quirky novels of the Scottish *Muriel SPARK* (b. 1918), most famously *The Prime of Miss Jean Brodie* (1961). Meanwhile, Murdoch's Irish compatriot *William TREVOR* (b. 1928) wrote the kind of finely crafted stories that give social realism a good name.

Writer's writer
Through a long period, the most loved of all authors among London's literary establishment was V. S. Pritchett because his turn of phrase was so felicitous, and his humor and sense of character so generous; also because his short stories and memoirs, based on his deep knowledge of London life, were intimate in scale and lacked imposing pretensions.

One Fat Englishman: Kingsley Amis poses to publicize one of his later titles.

1961 The drug thalidomide, prescribed to pregnant women, is found to cause malformations in their babies.

1962 American movie star and icon Marilyn Monroe dies of a drug overdose.

1964 Nelson Mandela is imprisoned for life in South Africa's notorious Robben Island jail, charged with conspiring to overthrow the government.

1960s
A Thing About Things
Experimentalism

Would it help to talk about things? No, I mean things. *Pebbles, paperclips, plungers … Don't you see, we live in a world of* things. *This orange, for instance: it's so … it's so … well,* orange. *(I was going to say "like a setting sun"; but no! that would detract from its sheer orangeyness!)*

Sorry. I'm just trying to point you down a path traveled more than once in 20th-century writing. Firstly in New Jersey, by *William Carlos WILLIAMS* (1883–1963), who splits from his friend Pound (see p. 88) to devote himself singlemindedly to the particulars of life—flowers, fruit, feelings that came to him, poems on the page (for they themselves are objects)—and to throw every sort of symbolism out the window. Williams' "objectivism" (winning in small poems, wearisome over the length of *Paterson*, 1946–51) is developed in the early 1930s by Louis Zukofsky—who turns to the idea of poems as objects of *sound*, and who in turn helps to inspire

"A Doctor Writes." New Jersey medic William Carlos Williams. He said his profession gave him access to "the secret gardens of the self."

the Black Mountain poets of the mid-1950s (see p. 132).

Switch to Paris, about the same time. *Alain ROBBE-GRILLET* (b. 1922) wakes up to the fact that fiction is, well, *fiction*. Novels are objects of printed paper that resemble nothing but themselves; they aren't a bit like life; it's only your imagination that makes you suppose they are. His *nouveau roman* (e.g. *Dans le labyrinthe*, 1960) sets out, through disruptions and trails leading nowhere, to jolt the reader into recognition of these bracing *aperçus*. (Do I detect a whiff of sarcasm, even *ennui*?—Ed.) Conferring with R-G in this project are Michel Butor—who turns "texts" into one-off sculptural

MEMO

Experimentalism in England has a small but distinguished base: the fine-tuned fictions of Gabriel Josipovici (also a superb critic) and of Christine Brooke-Rose, and the glum but often very funny novels of B. S. Johnson.

1965 Bohumil Hrabal's novel, *Closely Observed Trains*, shows little people caught up in incomprehensible events.

1967 Elvis Presley marries Priscilla Beaulieu, causing hysteria among his fans.

1969 Charles Manson and 23 of his followers are arrested following a series of gruesome murders in Los Angeles.

objects—and Nathalie Sarraute, an independent experimentalist reaching for the "tropisms" of behavior that lie below speech. Francis Ponge, another poet with a thing about things, shares the same spirit, as do the "concrete poets" of the 1960s, who resuscitated the typographical experiments of Guillaume Apollinaire.

Does this all sound distinctly esoteric? Out of the same experimental stable, however, come two authors with a more general appeal. *Marguerite DURAS* (1914–96), lyrically recircling her words, dropping all explanations, creates musings on love and death that grab an enduring audience—largely through the sense that this was a new, and specifically feminist, voice in writing.

Georges PEREC (1936–82)—a word-juggler famous for the fiendish cleverness that produced the novel without the letter "e," *La Disparition* (1969), and its successor with no other vowel, *Les Révénences*—uses such dry structural principles to write a huge and hugely generous masterpiece. *La Vie: Mode d'emploi* (1987)—in which an apartment block becomes a cornucopia of stories, ranging from the hilarious to the melancholy—that lives up to its title: a metaphor for life.

Weird words, weird beard: Perec with the Russian writer Zinoviev in 1978.

1950-53 When South Korea is invaded by North Korea, aided and abetted by the USSR and Communist China, a U.S.-dominated United Nations coalition enters the fray.

1962 American folk singer Bob Dylan writes "Blowin' in the Wind."

1964 Martin Luther King becomes *Time* magazine's Man of the Year and, the same year, the youngest Nobel Peace Prize winner.

1960s~1980s

GAN Warfare
Star Spotting

The Naked and the Dead.

The U.S. may hanker after the GAN, but what it really wants is the GAW. The Writer Superstar! Let's talk about Norman MAILER (b. 1923). Let's talk about him because that's what he likes us doing, and it's better than plowing through his books. O.K., the first of these, The Naked and the Dead *back in 1948, is a powerful war novel, and* The Executioner's Song *(1979) is an example of brilliant journalism.*

The Great Australian Novel
The golden wallaby has to rest with Patrick White, another deeply purposeful artist with conflicting, even tragic feelings concerning Australia. These are expressed in the steely, commanding prose of *The Tree of Man* (1955) and *Voss* (1957), each stories of loners pitting themselves against the continent, but in very different settings; White's range of material, over five decades of novel writing, is enormous.

But Mailer the great brawler, the pundit, the lover! The man who stabbed his wife (charges dropped) while he ran for mayor of New York; who was the hero of the Vietnam demos; who astonished the world by slamming out a thousand pages on pharaonic Egypt (*Ancient Evenings,* 1987; mostly rubbish)— ah, now that's what I call a writer!

The film of Truman Capote's early novel *Breakfast at Tiffany's.* Any excuse will do for a picture of Audrey Hepburn.

Not like that WASPy wimp *John UPDIKE* (b. 1932), stuck at his desk diligently scribbling his fancy prose about commuter-belt wife-swapping (*Couples*) and his oh-so-tidy nods at everything within the worldly-wise conspectus of the *New York Review of Books.* Or his forebear in smart suburban word-spinning, *John CHEEVER* (1912–82). Hey, but isn't Updike's *Rabbit* (1960–90) series actually the best report on

1965 Mao Tse-Tung introduces China's Cultural Revolution, a far-reaching reform movement involving the elimination of opposition, political and intellectual.

1968 Revolts by students and workers in France nearly topple de Gaulle's government.

1974 Solzhenitsyn is expelled from Russia after publication of *The Gulag Archipelago*.

middle America of its times? And can that Updike write sex!

Report, did you say? If you want the facts, go to Truman Capote's *In Cold Blood* (1966). Faction, man. It's the new thing. Invention's so passé. It's all a matter of tapping at that keyboard, and just being who you are. If you're a cool kinda guy, that is, like CAPOTE (1924–84)—or Tom Wolfe, or Hunter S. Thompson.

Yeah, but just being who you are—it ain't that simple, if you're a Jewish brainbox with Mamma, Yahweh, and Saul Bellow at your back, and more trouble in store down your pants. But that's great, y'know? I mean, to get the measure of contemporary reality you gotta be complex—adopt multiple personas—argue between them; you gotta be as smart as Philip Roth (yes, he of *Portnoy's Complaint*, 1969), I mean, he's the guy who's actually written *The Great American Novel* (1981)!

Oh, let's not talk about Americans, just for a change. Let's talk about the modest charms of British fiction, about the clever, unpretentious thrillers of Len Deighton, the small but beautifully formed novels of Penelope Fitzgerald (e.g. *Offshore*, 1980), or the sober probity of Paul Bailey (*Gabriel's Lament*, 1980) … Let's not think too hard about the faintly portentous John LeCarré, and avoid altogether the unbearably self-satisfied Anthony Burgess. Rather Mailer than him.

Beat

The smack-and-sodomy world of William Burroughs makes dull reading, worsened by his notorious "cut-up" technique; Jack Kerouac's *On the Road* (1957) is a soggy, so-so ramble. But hey,

Ginsberg performs.

those guys were cool … so put their stuff on your shelf, and read the biogs. Too late, now, to hear their ally Allen Ginsberg do his poetic stuff in person—but, as with other American poets of this 1950s generation (e.g. Kenneth Rexroth in San Francisco, Frank O'Hara in New York), live performance was the heart of the matter.

Beat buddies Neal Cassady and Jack Kerouac.

1960 The Student Nonviolent Coordinating Committee (SNCC) is founded in the U.S., to work for civil rights in the Deep South.

1966 In Rome, the office of Inquisitor is abolished.

1967 Civil war breaks out in Nigeria when the state of Biafra secedes. About one million people will have died of starvation by 1970.

1960s~1970s

Just Because You're Paranoid . . .
Reclusive Americans

J. D. Salinger, prereclusive.

… it doesn't mean that they're not out to get you. We all know that. We know it thanks to a line of American novelists who made the contest of mad loner with even madder system a prime theme in American fiction between the 1960s and 1980s: the era of MAD, Mutually Assured (thermonuclear) Destruction.

Their forerunner is *J. D. SALINGER* (b. 1919), famed for the winning teenager-against-the-phonies immediacy of *The Catcher in the Rye* (1951) and for little else apart from his determination (paranoid, no doubt) to spend his latter years as a recluse. But, for the broad public, the definitive statement of the screwiness of "the system" came with *Catch–22* (1961), Joseph Heller's black-humor exposé of military absurdity. After the huge impact of this book, *HELLER* (b. 1923) likewise sulked reclusively for 13 years—eventually returning more in the Bellow mode of Jewish American wiseacre with *Something Happened* (1974) and *God Knows* (1984). Rueful, witty wisdom about a grotesque world was also the mode of *Kurt VONNEGUT* (b. 1922), who, like Heller, achieved fame with a late version of

the WWII novel, *Slaughterhouse Five* (1969), though his earlier *Cat's Cradle* (1963), more firmly embedded in science fiction, shows off his engaging persona at its best.

The supremo of paranoia, however, was Thomas Pynchon. The author's zeal

Heller's *Catch-22*, filmed in 1970, directed by Mike Nichols.

1967 The Sexual Offences Act is passed in Great Britain, decriminalizing homosexual acts between consenting adults.

1974 British peer Lord Lucan disappears; he is suspected of killing his children's nanny and seriously injuring his wife.

1977 Woody Allen directs *Annie Hall*, starring his one-time partner Diane Keaton.

Sci-fi: dry

Paranoia naturally bridges "real life" (whatever that is) and classic, dry science fiction. In that genre, Frederick Pohl's story "The Tunnel under the World" (1954) is a perfect nutshell statement of the theme. The brilliantly various Philip K. Dick explored what would happen if each person's world were entirely self-enclosed in *Eye in the Sky* (1957) and *Ubik* (1969). The central SF theme of aliens—i.e., where intelligence parts company with humanity—had its finest expositor in the Pole Stanislaw Lem (b. 1921).

in covering his traces has correspondingly increased his standing as a legend. His weightily mysterious debut, *V.* (1963), a complex allegory about albino alligators in the sewers of New York, was followed by *The Crying of Lot 49* (1966), which elegantly sets out the conundrum that either the world means something (and probably means no good toward you)—or that it's all in your head and things mean nothing, but that there can be no certainty which. *Gravity's Rainbow* (1973) is anything but elegant— a colossal pile of smoldering, deliquescent information concerning the ending of WWII, emitting hallucinogenic vapors and eventually collapsing under its own weight—but in this very irresolubility it still stands, for every geek of "the information age," as the great novel of its times. Later Pynchons (after the long silence obligatory to writers in this mode) are more modest in scope.

Paranoia was taken by many American critics for literary seriousness—because it

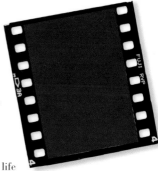

The nearest we got to a recent photograph of Thomas Pynchon. Born in 1930, Cornell-educated, navy trained—this is all the information in the public domain.

organized everything in life into a significance that might be delusory, and this uncertainty seemed to epitomize the problems of modern writing. The question "Does it all hang together?," present in the clever-clever academic experiments of John Barth (*Giles Goat-Boy*, 1966) and the much funnier anti-novels of Donald Barthelme (*Snow White*, 1967), also weaves through the demanding fiction of William Gaddis (e.g. *Carpenter's Gothic*, 1985) and underpins Don DeLillo's end-of-century attempt at the GAN, *Underworld* (1997).

Sci-fi: wet

During the late 1960s, science fiction left off the dry, specs-and-shirtsleeves functionality of its "Golden Age" (*see* p. 108–9) and got poetic … sensitized … wet. The development's partly due to J. G. Ballard with *The Drowned World* (1962) and *High Rise* (1975) (see also page 126), but Ursula LeGuin (b. 1929), with her clutch of alternative, holistically uplifting universes, is largely responsible (*The Left Hand of Darkness*, 1969). More recently, William Gibson has led the field with his Virtual Reality dystopias (*Miracle Worker*, 1984; *Mona Lisa Overdrive*, 1989, and *Neuromancer*, 1995).

1960 Quasars, the most luminous known objects in the universe, are detected.

1963 Building on British experiments revealing the principle of holography, American scientists demonstrate holograms using laser technology.

1964 The construction of Stonehenge is explained as a means of predicting lunar eclipses.

1960s~1970s

Pataphysical Jacarandas
The South Americans

In the later 20th century, South America, otherwise a bit-part continent on the global stage, was famed for three great exports: soccer players, cocaine, and "magic realism." The brains behind the last of these concepts is Jorge Luis BORGES (1899–1986; behind whom, Machado de Assis—see p. 87) and the writer who did the most to bring it worldwide renown is Gabriel GARCÍA MÁRQUEZ (b. 1928).

La belle Isabel, niece of the president of Chile who was assassinated in 1973.

Borges, whose chief work was done in Buenos Aires back in the 1930s and 40s, is the most reader-friendly of all the great subversive, modernist rethinkers of literature—because he takes so little of the reader's time. His short parables—a few pages long, sometimes just a paragraph—contain more imagination-bending ideas (and more wisdom) than whole libraries-full of the literary erudition and philosophy they reflect; they are also prose of a wonderfully image-rich, poised elegance. Collected (e.g. in *Labyrinths*, 1962), they form a master key to a new imaginative world.

Multiple choice

Cortázar's *Hopscotch* is the prototype for a host of "you-decide" fictional formats that have arrived in the computer age. Click for the conclusion that makes you happy. This line may yet produce really exciting reading experiences— but, as with so many other invitations to be truly democratic (forgive my cynicism), participant fiction seems like too much hassle for too trivial rewards.

Julio CORTÁZAR (b. 1914), also an Argentine intellectual but one hilariously despairing about intellectuality, boldly stepped into this new world with *Hopscotch* (1963)—the chapters of which you are invited to shuffle and read in any order you choose, constructing alternative

1967 Latin American revolutionary and guerrilla leader Che Guevara is killed in Bolivia.

1970 Marxist leader Salvadore Allende is elected president of Chile.

1978 In Tanzania, footprints thought to have been made by a human ancestor 3.6 million years ago are found.

stories. At the same time, the Cuban novelist *Alejo* CARPENTIER (1904–80) was putting forward the Latin American writer's predicament as a challenge—to express what had never been expressed, the "marvelous real" that was their native environment. Join these two and you get the formula: (mind-bending narrative experiments) + (brilliantly bizarre local color) = magic realism.

The product that sold this formula to the wide world—one of the crucial novels of the later 20th century—is *One Hundred Years of Solitude* (1967), by the Colombian Gabriel García Márquez. Its imaginary town of Macondo, where ghosts coexist with all-too-palpable poverty and where the rains will fall without cease for four years, stands for a basic South American reality which swirls and shifts in phantasmagoric extravagance. The

THE PLOT THICKENS

Brazil's most popular storyteller of the 1960s and 1970s, **Clarice Lispector,** *has only tenuous links with magic realism. She has a quirky, questioning mode of lyrical introspection, but as a Ukrainian Jewish immigrant with a sharply sardonic take on everything, she stood apart from other Portuguese writers. Recommended:* Family Ties *(1960).*

novel would also define fictional parameters for writers the world over in the next 30 years (see pp. 126–27).

In *Solo Century*'s wake (Márquez would write other, equally remarkable novels), writers of outrageous flair and panache seemed to sprout up all over Latin America: Carlos Fuentes in Mexico, fusing myth and history with stupendous vigor in *Terra Nostra* (1975); Mario Vargas Llosa, loftily surveying the social diversities and disparities of Peru; Augusto Roa Bastos, with his intimidating encyclopedia of Paraguay, *I the Supreme* (1974); and most popular of all, Isabel Allende, transmuting the terrors and passions of Chile into *The House of the Spirits* (1985).

The theorist to all this writing, but more importantly a great and deeply thoughtful poet, is the Mexican *Octavio* PAZ (b. 1914).

To see the world as if through untutored eyes: naïve paintings like this one by Tamas Galambos demonstrate "Magic Realist" values.

1963 Astronaut John Glenn survives unhurt after his space capsule catches fire on reentry to Earth's atmosphere and plummets into the Atlantic Ocean.

1967 The British Blasphemy Law (1697) is repealed by the Criminal Law Act.

1970 *Sexual Politics* by Kate Millett, an influential feminist text, argues that relations between the sexes are governed by the male need to retain power over women.

1960s~1980s

From the Fabs to Fabulism
The Nature of Fiction

What's too close blurs in the vision; it's too early to write the literary history of the late 20th century. But the next few pages pick out some shapes that seem to loom in it.

One is the turn away from European postwar realism that dates from Grass' *Tin Drum* (see p. 115)—and also from Italo Calvino's move to a crazy, light-heartedly playful "meta-fiction" (on the jolly side of arid in the minitrilogy *Our Ancestors*, 1960). It's the tide that would turn the Czech Milan Kundera, an anti-Stalinist realist in the passionate sadness and humor of *The Joke* (1967), into the paradoxical philosopher of *The Unbearable Lightness of Being* (1984).

This same drift ran through English writing in the mind-bending decade of the Beatles and hippiedom. John Fowles, in *The Magus* (1963) and *The French Lieutenant's Woman* (1969), played—invitingly, but irresolutely—with the fictional nature of fiction, while Doris Lessing, originally depicting colonial life, bypassed accepted social realities in the books that ran from the great feminist consciousness raiser, *The Golden Notebook* (1962), to the dazzling, visionary *Memoirs of a Survivor* (1974). From this point she moved into science fiction. (The Canadian Margaret Atwood took a comparable path.) The most memorable images of 1960s British fiction come from the poetic apocalypses of *J.G. BALLARD* (b. 1930).

Doris Lessing in the 1990s. She was brought up in Southern Rhodesia.

> ### THE PLOT THICKENS
>
> *English poetry: 1920s Eliot modernist mythic; 1930s Auden political; 1940s Dylan Thomas apocalyptic; 1950s Larkin Movement low-key; 1960s Plath confessional. O.K., say* **John Fuller** *and* **James Fenton** *(followed by the feeble* **Craig Raine***), we'll do a new mood for the 1970s, we'll be flip, fun, ludic! File under: Post-modernism, minor manifestations. Admire: Fenton's German Requiem and Staffordshire Murderer.*

1977 The rare cancer Kaposi's sarcoma is diagnosed in two homosexual men, thought to be the first cases of AIDS in the U.S.

1980 Fiber optics, which use hair-thin strands of flexible glass and light-emitting diodes or lasers to transmit telephone and television signals, are developed.

1988 The new wonder drug Prozac is approved for treatment of depression.

Post-structuralism

(Structuralism simple you got on p. 119.) P-S, or "deconstruction," or "critical theory," was the child of Sorbonne prof Jacques Derrida, and an infant much beloved of academe. It held up the cat's cradle of cultural "structures," which was supposed by its predecessors to cradle the cat of "reality," and exclaimed that there was "no damn cat, no damn cradle" (as Kurt Vonnegut once put it). Words were always about to mean something but never fully did in themselves; all you could talk about was the chance of meaning shifting along the line in "différence." Ah, but how you could talk about it! (And the long words you could use!) The opportunities that were opened up for supercilious, smart-ass academic self-justification!

All this—what shall we say?—turn to the weird received a massive boost from the example of Borges and Márquez (see pp. 124–25), not to mention Bulgakov (see p. 97). The result was a new, synthetic standard acceptable fictional world.

This world is stocked with colorful, interestingly offbeat objects and flocks of fancy adjectives. Bodies wander among them, feeling and fucking their way around: they may bear kooky names and deformities, but they are rarely burdened with old-fashioned characters. (They are kind of *post*-character.) Their actions slither in and out of dream mode, history mode (tons of that), this-is-the-writer-writing mode, rarely holding with tenacity to any particular assertion about reality (because this is postmodernism—or it's one of the meanings of that over-worked catchword).

You want examples? Try reading the intriguingly pretentious novels of Michel Tournier (*The Erl-King*, 1979) or Umberto Eco's affably spurious bestseller, *The Name of the Rose* (1980); Patrick Süskind's *Perfume* (1985), another ingenious pastiche of the past; Orhan Pamuk, the inventive Turk (*The New Life*, 1997), and Juan Goytisolo, the fantastical Spaniard (*Makbara*, 1980). Or try Christoph Ransmayr doing Ovid's exile in *The Last World* (1988).

More to Anglophone tastes, more fact-and-character-fixed: the prodigal Australian Peter Carey (*Oscar and Lucinda*, 1988), and Louis de Bernières, who wrote Britain's favorite book of the 1990s in *Captain Corelli's Mandolin* (1994). "Fabulism," that's the accepted moniker. Time to draw a line under it?

Liz Wright's *Jaguar Hunter*: an example of Magic Realism exported.

1984 Scientists at the University of California, Berkeley, clone genes from an extinct animal, the zebralike quagga. What next—dinosaurs?

1985 The British Antarctic Survey detects a hole in the ozone layer over Antarctica.

1986 The European Space Agency's Giotto spacecraft comes within 335 miles of Halley's Comet.

1980s

Mutilation Chic
Punks and Yuppies

The 1980s, like the 1920s and the 1960s, but unlike the century's other segments, was a decade in love with itself. Or more exactly: caught in a queasy fascination with its own lurid, swaggering hubris. Money, violence, and excess became favorite themes for writers on both sides of the Atlantic.

1980s urban realism by Jock McFadyean: *The Love Bite*. Frantic deadlines, city chaos, and the violent side of lust.

*M*oney (1984) fueled this fascination; *London Fields* (1989) finalized it. The two books pullulate with details of the decade's linguistic, stylistic, and financial excesses, and *Martin Amis* (b.1949; son of Kingsley A., see p. 116), unlike most of the folks on the last page, had a knack for fusing them into unforgettable characters. As fashion moves elsewhere, readers will cringe at the half-digested science that Amis chews on, even if they don't at his stylistic rip-offs from Bellow; but these remain fat landmarks of their times

(along, of course, with Tom Wolfe's formula GAN for the 1980s, *Bonfire of the Vanities*, 1988).

Like much concurrent writing, Amis' books feed on a spiky, grotesque sensibility that came to the foreground in the wake of late 1970s

The mutilated monologue

A solitary male voice, muttering and cursing to itself and somehow through its bleary waywardness reflecting the way of the world around it: this pitch, which starts with Beckett, was taken up by the Russian Viktor Erofeev (*Moscow Circles*, 1977) and more recently—and with great tenderness and flair—by the Scottish James Kelman (*A Disaffection*, 1989). Compare the wonderfully bad-tempered musings of Thomas Bernhard concerning his native Austria.

1987 Primo Levi commits suicide shortly after finishing his final book about the Holocaust.

1990 Launch of the Game Boy portable computer game.

1995 The Tate Gallery in London exhibits Damien Hirst's *Mother and Child Divided*—glass tanks in which a cow and her calf are displayed cut in half.

THE PLOT THICKENS

Iain Sinclair is by far the most distinctive voice among an array of lyricists-cum-satirists of fin-de-siècle British life. He conjures up a lurid, occult, obsessional London in prose of glutted, contorted brilliance. (Though Downriver, *1993, is not everyone's idea of a novel-type novel.) A hidden, alternative London is also the theme of* Vale Royal, *1994, the masterwork of* **Andrew Aidan Dun,** *currently Britain's most exciting poet-performer.*

punk rock. The early stories of Ian McEwan, cooly turning over gross and morbid material (*In Between the Sheets*, 1978), contribute to it; its sharpest exponents would be the Scots Iain Banks and Irvine Welsh, though the New Yorker Bret Easton Ellis also had—well, a "stab"—in his *American Psycho* (1991), at this mutilation chic.

Mutilation was a favorite fictional image because it connected with the academic trend for theorizing "the body" (such a handy peg for blather about gender, ethnicity, and relativism), and with the lead from Burroughs picked up by writers like Kathy Acker. But it had also—ring by ring, stud by stud—simply become an observable facet of contemporary culture. Like the other jagged edges that these writers fingered—smack, porno, etc.—it was material for a contemporary version of realism. Ellis' protagonist switches between butchery and boutiques—where he rejoins the yuppie company described by other writers of the mid-1980s New York "bratpack," such as Jay McInerney (*Bright Lights Big City*, 1984).

Yuppiedom—which was smug or it was nothing—got its most charming self-flattery in Vikram Seth's *The Golden Gate* (1986). Though Seth boldly adopted Pushkin's "verse novel" mode (equally adroitly, he would marry the leisure of the European 19th-century novel to 1950s middle-class India in *A Suitable Boy*, 1993, and sell it), the stuff of his writing was love tangles, domestic particulars, evocations of place—terrain he shared with a thousand quietly excellent contemporary novelists (too many to start naming). The broad, inviting middle ground, in fact, of the novel ever since Fielding.

Martin Amis, seen awaiting dental treatment. He is notorious for demanding gargantuan advances to finance his obsession with ivory revival.

1983 In Iran, Ayatollah Khomeini, declaring Islam to be "a religion of the sword," sends armed pilgrims to Mecca.

1988 Film maker Krzysztof Kieslowski's *Dekalog* imaginatively reexamines the Ten Commandments in contemporary Poland.

1989 2,000 prodemocracy demonstrators are killed in Tiananmen Square in Beijing when army tanks are sent in.

1980s~1990s

Border Incidents
The Dispossessed

Solzhenitsyn after his long-delayed return to Russia in the 1990s.

On February 14, 1989, the back-stabbing, contract-grabbing, inward-turned community of Western writing received its biggest shock of the postwar period — and, in a sense, its biggest compliment — when the Ayatollah Khomeini, concluding his leadership of Iran with a vicious dying kick, called for the murder of one of its members.

Never mind that the occasion of the fatwa was a petulant cheap shot at the Prophet Muhammad brought in to enliven *The Satanic Verses* (1988), Salman Rushdie's most turgid novel. Here was a major literary star having to hide for his life in Great Britain. Writing, and the freedom of the imagination, once again mattered—life-and-death mattered.

And this just at the point when—what with the fall of the Berlin Wall and the dissident playwright Vaclav Havel becoming president of Czechoslovakia—prospects from east to west looked equally writer-friendly, and equally bland. Gone were the Cold War days when *Aleksandr Solzhenitsyn* (b.1918) had towered on the world's moral stage, a bastion of righteousness against Soviet tyranny. Eventually returning to Russia from his exile, he would be cut down to size as just another name on the shelf, and (excepting *One Day in the Life of Ivan Denisovich*, 1962, which briefly took Khrushchev's fancy) a rather dull one at that.

But for others in the postcolonial era, exile and dislocation would remain central to the fabric of experience —none more so than Rushdie (b. 1947), who built the swirling, sprawling, tumblingly vivacious bizarrerie of his fiction (outstandingly, *Midnight's Children*, 1981) on the tension

Márquez as well: see p. 125). Much writing
of the 1980s and 1990s trod this frontier
ground—for instance, the Chinese
Californian novels of Amy Tan and Maxine
Hong Kingston, the Afro-Caribbean
history novels of Caryl Phillips and David
Dabydeen, or the Anglo-Asian comedy of
Hanif Kureishi or I. Allan Sealy. The shift
of ethnic and cultural boundaries explored
by these writers was also echoed sexually
by gay writers like Aldo Busi, Edmund
White, and David Leavitt.

Like blocks built where the Berlin Wall
had stood, new classics rose up out of all
this borderland writing. *Toni MORRISON*
(b. 1931) brought together the unwritten
history of African Americans in a
compelling series of novels—*Song
of Solomon* (1977), *Tar
Baby* (1981), *Beloved*
(1987)—whose
commanding rhythmic
prose and emotional
boldness placed her
center stage as the
Great American Writer
for her times. And
unexpectedly, for the
first time since Hardy,
rural southern England
became the material of
a masterpiece, as
V. S. Naipaul (see p.
115) mused on his own
immigré's approach to it in the majestic
prose of *The Enigma of Arrival* (1987).

THE PLOT THICKENS

The Satanic Verses *(in my opinion)*
abused Muhammad, whom Muslims
love; and if you insult someone I love,
I've a right to express my hurt (though
not to kill you), and for you to talk
about "literature" is irrelevant. BUT:
Rushdie's imperilment, despite the
lifting of the fatwa in 1998, is at the
forefront of cases all over the world
where writers are threatened by
governments or interests who can't
stand the freedom of imagination or
the risk of truth; and if those things
matter, we ought to support the cause
he represents.

A demonstration against Salman Rushdie in Peshawar, North Pakistan. Both protestors and advocates lost their lives over *The Satanic Verses*.

1965 The first fully commercial communications satellite (*Early Bird*) is launched into synchronous orbit.

1978 Bulgarian defector Georgi Markov is killed with a poisoned umbrella.

1984 Indian troops lay siege to the Golden Temple at Amritsar, where Sikh extremists have barricaded themselves.

1960s~1998

Do Wide Margins Mean Marginal?

Contemporary Poets

What's the point of all that writing that doesn't reach the end of the page, these days? There are lots of answers to that one: let's pick out four, and use them as points on a compass to try to map the complexities of contemporary poetry: "Page," who said "page?" goes one argument. "Poetry is a living **voice**, *it's the whole sound of who I am …" This is to paraphrase a drift of thought that stems from Zukofsky (see p. 118) and thence through Charles Olson's 1950s "Black Mountain" disciples to meet up with "confessional" verse (see p. 113). It's an argument that leads out of the realm of written literature, into performance—which is where poetry started, after all. But its impact has been felt on the page as well as the stage during the last 40 years.*

Tone to conscience
Derek Walcott, fine-phrasing the West Indies; Derek Mahon, superb laconic Irishman; Miroslav Holub, humanely rational Czech; Frederick Seidel, civilized but haunted New Yorker; Brian Hinton, English polemic wit.

Voice to tone
Sharon Olds, American woman's experience; Yevgeny Yevtushenko, Soviet Russia's favorite exportable good guy; Tony Harrison, rumbustious Yorkshire ranter; Linton Kwesi Johnson, righteous Black British.

"**P**oetry," goes a contrasting view, "is the conscience of our civilization. It's the fullest **consciousness** of our history and language, of our predicament." This is a type of modernist argument that ultimately derives from Eliot and Pound (see p. 88), but it also relates to poets who think of their work politically, as speech for and from a certain community. In English poetry, the key example is the demanding but magnificent work of *Geoffrey* HILL. At his worst, Hill (b.1932) sounds like Eliot with constipation, but at best he offers the unique, heady excitement of language at maximum charge: it is, simply, great poetry.

Derek Walcott, the lyricist of St. Lucia. His work deals with West Indian identity and culture.

1991 When Croatia, then Bosnia-Herzegovina (1992), secedes from Yugoslavia, Slobodan Milosevic backs Serbian insurgents, unleashing bitter conflict.

1995 26-year-old Nick Leeson is accused of causing the collapse of Barings Bank after running up losses of £620 million in the futures market.

1998 Poet Ted Hughes breaks a 30-year silence and publishes *Birthday Letters*, poems exploring his relationship with Sylvia Plath. He died later that year.

Conscience to space

Les Murray, Australia's big man for God and nature; Pauline Stainer, chillily mystical, honorably English; Yves Bonnefoy, Philippe Jaccottet, beautiful metaphysical French; R. S. Thomas, tough-minded Welsh vicar.

"Famous Seamus," Ireland's most-loved man of letters, searches for the perfect words.

Two intermediate, more reader-friendly positions between the two above: "Poetry cleanses your perceptions: it opens up the space of imaginative truth, and shows you it." An argument that has long applied both to poetry of nature and locality and to metaphysical speculation: in the 20th century, its supreme exemplar is Rilke. Or, alternatively: "Poetry offers you a companionable tone, an attitude with which to negotiate this tricky contemporary world." Which is what poets from Horace to Auden have done, a task continued by the English-writing Russian expat *Joseph BRODSKY* (b.1940) and the Irishman Derek Mahon, and attempted (indifferently on the whole) by most of the poets who have come to the fore in 1990s Britain.

You can take these as the N, S, E, and W of poetry's compass, and play at arranging recent poets between them (as I've done in the boxes). Really, however, all these directions meet and match. Who I am involves what this civilization is, and vice versa. Finding what's out there in the world involves finding a tone of feeling to invoke it, as poets like *Seamus HEANEY*

(b. 1939) or Amy Clampitt show. In fact most worthwhile contemporary poets could rise to any of these requirements; moreover, they can offer you the incidental pleasure of watching words come together surely and beautifully.

Space to voice

Elizabeth Bishop (1911–79) (whom we should have discussed before; big influence on fellow Americans); John Ashbery, affably wafty New Yorker; Thom Gunn (b.1929), clear-headed, fine-crafted, open-hearted English American immigrant. And millions more, beyond naming... Maybe including you?

1990 East and West Germany are reunited and fireworks light the sky over Berlin.

1991 First publication of Jung Chang's *Wild Swans*, the story of three generations of Chinese women that will dominate the bestseller lists for years.

1993 The Human Genome Project is launched in San Diego to map the key genes in the body and figure out what they do.

1980s~2000

It's My Story and I'll Cry If I Want To
Fictional Autobiography

The twentieth century ends— and what a sad affair it's been, looking back. Examining its horrors, so it seems, has been one of the chief concerns of writers in its final years.

Many of them have taken their cue from *Primo LEVI* (1919–87). Levi, steady, humane, and sober, looked for ways to ponder his own witnessing of Auschwitz in the series of books that reached from *If This Is a Man* (1947) to *The Drowned and the Saved* (1986), finished just before his suicide. Another Jewish survivor of near-incommunicable atrocities, *Aharon APPELFELD* (b. 1932), evoked his childhood experiences, and his own distance from them as an adult writer, with a spare obliqueness in *The Age of Wonders* (1978) and *The Healer* (1985). Yet more oblique, but equally haunting and poignant, was the alternative-world mode adopted by Dan Jacobson in his compact masterpiece, *The God-fearer* (1992).

Remarkably, perhaps, the urge to write about the Holocaust seemed to increase the further the event receded in time. Its memory lay behind two of the most admired books of the 1990s, Anne Michaels's

> ### THE PLOT THICKENS
>
> *Some of the finest realist fiction of the 1990s has been conceived on a grand, expansive scale:* **Rohinton Mistry's** *panoramic tale of 1970s India,* A Fine Balance *(1995), and* **Jane Smiley's** *family saga* A Thousand Acres *(1994). As against this, there has been a trend for compact, well-mannered restraint. Instances: many of the books on this page, or* **Ian McEwan's** *later novels* (Enduring Love, *1997), or* **Steven Milhauser's** *American parable,* Martin Dressler *(1997).*

How it *wasn't.* Soviet painter Deineka glosses over the millions lost in war.

1994 Former U.S. president Ronald Reagan announces that he has Alzheimer's disease.

1995 The highest life expectancy in the world is in Japan, where men live for an average of 81.6 years and women 75.9.

1996 Controversy flares over cases of "recovered memory" when people remember incidents of childhood abuse.

Fugitive Pieces (1996) and Bernhard Schlink's *The Reader* (1996). At the same time, yet more distant memories were being exhumed in many of the decade's bestsellers—for instance the echoes of World War I that reverberated in the books of Pat Barker and Sebastian Faulks in England, or Jean Rouaud in France.

To remember. From 1943, the paperwork of genocide.

Indeed, the business of remembering—with one foot planted on fact, the other dangling in fantasy—came to the foreground of writing in the era of "false memory syndrome." It was reflected in the device of the "unreliable narrator," as used for instance in the elegantly melancholy

novels of Kazuo Ishiguro. The "faction" of Capote (see p. 131), moreover, had taken firm root; novels regularly alleged that the events they described had actually occurred.

The stuff of storytelling had typically come to be what happened to me (and did it, or did I only think it did?) and what happened to my folks (and would they mind if I told you?). Seamus Deane's *Reading in the Dark* (1997) and W. G. Sebald's *The Emigrants* (1996) are fine examples. Like Schlink's book and like *The Border Trilogy* and Cormac McCarthy's other novels of the American West, they are written with a coolly distinguished eloquence that's one of the more refreshing tones

From the film of Capote's *In Cold Blood* (see p. 121), precursor to much writing of the 1990s.

of the 1990s (following hot-headed fabulism). But there's something rather sad (in all senses) about all these backward-turned heads.

2000: could it be time for some faith in the imagination?

Canonades

So there you have it: the complete and total history of literature, 3,000-odd years in 62 easy spreads. Which leaves us a couple of pages in which to run over the perennial chestnuts of literary argumentation.

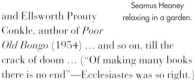

Read me, saith Vikram.

Seamus Heaney relaxing in a garden.

Pronounced One-upmanship

The real mark of *Crash Course* competence in Literature. Take a tip from the natives: it's Vladimir NaBOKov (not Nab–a–cough). Roland BARTEZ (not Barfs). SalMAHN Rushdie. Fernando PESHWAH (Pessoa). "My scene, ass" and the E. Knee Idd. Horhay Luis Borhaze, Sezar Vayekho, Don Keyhotay—surely, I don't need to spell all this out? But these little things count for much more than having read all the books, you may be sure.

B ut hang on—I can hear you saying—how come no mention of *Fanny FERN* (1811–72) the seminal feminist and *Eino LEINO* (1878–1926) the felicitous Finn (sorry: haven't read 'em), Julian Barnes and Paul Muldoon (simply: don't rate 'em), Mary Webb and Douglas Dunn (like 'em, but …), your frightfully talented friend Lavinia Pruitt, my even more talented friend Jan Siegel (watch this space), Harold Manhood, author of *Gay Agony* (1930),

and Ellsworth Prouty Conkle, author of *Poor Old Bongo* (1954) … and so on, till the crack of doom … ("Of making many books there is no end"—Ecclesiastes was so right.)

But answering that leads us straight into the hoariest problem of all: how to select which books matter: which books form "the canon." This is not quite the same as asking what makes books "good." Obviously, a book's good if it gives you something good—and the good we hope for from reading poetry and fiction usually ranges somewhere between warm relaxation and bracing stimulation. If a book's given us some such experience, we should think twice before letting the critics walk all over it with lofty dismissals.

Nevertheless, serious critics have a reason for doing this—as well as for recommending good books we

Beat boys: Cassady and Kerouac.

hadn't known. They are trying to prod, shape, and extend in new directions the culture that we share. We share that culture insofar as we—or our kids—all face the same inevitable limitations of exam reading lists and media "books" coverage. Deciding what goes into those tight spaces is where the critical choice of a "canon" really becomes important.

we read to get that sense of depth can always be a matter for critical argument; but if the goal of that argument is a "canon," then it's a worthwhile objective.

Georges Perec and beard (and Zinoviev).

One option for critics is to treat books as if they were all of equal value, since they can all be treated as objects of criticism. It's true, they can: you can think just as clever thoughts about Jeffrey Archer as about Edmund Spenser, and many critics influenced by "deconstruction" (see p. 127) have done so. But this approach massively short-changes consumers with a limited choice, handing them a culture that's flat—all breadth and no depth. A depth of literary history, of continuing engagement with certain authors and values, gives anchorage to our self-respect. Exactly which books

The Bottom Line

The words "reality" and "realism" have rattled around this brief history like dried-up theoretical peas. But for most of us most of the time, reality has a horribly financial ring.

How does literature figure as a way of making money? Badly, goes the received idea; and info from PEN, the international writers' organization, confirms it. The average writer in the U.S. made a mere $5,000 per annum from his or her exertions in 1990. Ah, but the average never reveals much about fields defined by individual excellence, like the arts or sport. How do the major contenders fare?

The Losers

Charles Monroe Sheldon (1896–1978): wrote the bestselling novel of all time, a Christian utopian fantasy called *In His Steps*. It sold 30 million copies worldwide; he had parted with the rights for a princely $75.

John Milton, of more lasting fame, sold away *Paradise Lost* for just £10.

Cervantes, despite producing an instant international bestseller, died in penury, terminally ripped off.

Of course, many writers shed it quicker than they earn it—**Balzac** and **Scott**, forever overstretched, and the gambler **Dostoyevsky**, did their utmost to die broke.

Then there are the publisher-shy—**Hopkins** or **Dickinson** for instance—who hide their light under a bushel for their next of kin to get rich on. Or conversely the willing victims of the vanity-publishing trade: their model must be **Proust**, who actually paid to have the early volumes of *A la recherche* … printed (although he was later to recoup).

Most of the writers we're talking about balance just about successfully between their desire for literary respectability and their desire for the megabucks made by fiction machines like Agatha Christie and Jeffrey Archer. Quite a few, like Shakespeare (early retirement at 47), have become very comfortably off indeed. But since an income from sales of verbiage tends to be erratic, they have always looked to supplementary sources:

PATRONS

The powers that be bankroll scribblers in the (not always realized) hope that this will reflect credit back on themselves. People remember Mæcenas for backing Horace; but do they think better of Charles II for making Dryden Poet Laureate, or care about Rilke's princesses of this and that, or revere the Rockefellers for funding Hart Crane?

In the 20th century, the whim of individuals largely gave way to state patronage—through arts councils, charitable foundations, and the like—which gave rise to open-ended questions about who had a right to such patronage, and by what standards their merits could be assessed.

PRIZES

The beauty contests of literature: they have increasingly glamorized literary culture ever since the first Nobel Prize for Literature was awarded to René-François Sully Prudhomme (who?) in 1901. The annual presentations chiefly reveal the mentalities of different committees:

Nobel

The Swedish scholars foregather. "Isn't it time we had an East African winner? A Belgian? A Bhutanese?" They repeatedly pick writers that no one from the country concerned rates as supreme, but a worthy internationalism is preserved.

1933 Ivan Alekseyevich Bunin (first Russian to win)

1945 Gabriela Mistral, Chile (first Latin American)

1956 Juan Ramón Jiménez (Spanish)

1962 John Steinbeck (American)

1964 Offered to Jean-Paul Sartre (French), who refused to accept it

1983 William Golding (British)

1984 Jaroslav Seifert (Czech)

1991 Nadine Gordimer (African)

Pulitzer

Since 1918, Americans have wavered between the epic national history and the exquisite short fable:

1937 *Gone with the Wind*, Margaret Mitchell

1975 *Humboldt's Gift*, Saul Bellow

1979 *The Stories of John Cheever*

1988 *Beloved*, Toni Morrison

1991 *Rabbit at Rest*, John Updike

1996 *Independence Day*, Richard A. Ford

Goncourt

Parisian mandarin taste is agreed, by most outside observers, to have taken a long descent from the sublime to the ridiculous since Proust was awarded the laurels in 1919.

1980 *La Jardon d'acclimation*, Yves Navarre

1984 *The Lover*, Marguerite Duras

1990 *Les Champs d'honneur*, Jean Rouault

1996 *Le Chasseur Zéro*, Pascale Roze

Booker

A clutch of London's literary-media types arm-wrestle to promote their respective buddies, then all write bitchy press pieces disassociating themselves from the bathetic outcome.

1978 *The Sea, The Sea*, Iris Murdoch

1981 *Midnight's Children*, Salman Rushdie

1986 *The Old Devils*, Kingsley Amis

1991 *The Famished Road*, Ben Okri

1993 *Paddy Clarke Ha Ha Ha*, Roddy Doyle

1997 *The God of Small Things*, Arundhati Roy

If these prizes fail to recognize your distinctive excellence, there are thousands of others that might: You could try
The Herb Barrett Award for Canadian haikus
The Rose Mary Crawshay Award for writing on Byron, Shelley, or Keats (but only by women)
The Carey Award for outstanding services to indexing; for which our nomination goes to the author of the following pages.

Index